DREAM
SCREW IT!

BY
GEOFFREY GOLDEN

ILLUSTRATIONS BY
SHING YIN KHOR
ELAN' TRINIDAD
REID PSALTIS
MARC PALM

A Parody By
THE DEVASTATOR
FUNNY BOOKS FOR HUMANS

Dedicated to Mom,
who loved taking us
to Disney World,
and to Dad,
who hates Florida
and everything in it.

WRITTEN BY GEOFFREY GOLDEN
COVER ART: Spencer Dina
INTERIOR ART: Shing Yin Khor, Elan' Trinidad, Reid Psaltis, Marc Palm
Featuring Zach Ames as "Dipp Disney" and Justin Michael as "Morton Boggs"
DESIGN: Mike Reddy
EDITOR: Amanda Meadows
PHOTOGRAPHY: Aaron Alpert
HAIR AND MAKE-UP: Karina Caro

PHOTO CREDITS:
Wikimedia Commons users Coolcaesar, NASA, Florida Photographic Collection,
United States Congress, Ed Schipul, Alan Light, Ciccone39, Minnesota Historical Society Collections

Flickr users Justin Gurbisz, Orange County Archives, Children's Bureau Centennial,
Ron Cogswell, Global Reactions, Barbara Ann Spengler, Sam Howzit, ludovic

Copyright © 2016 Geoffrey Golden and The Devastator

ISBN-10:1942099126
ISBN-13: 978-1942099-12-3
First Edition: September 2016
devastatorpress.com

PRINTED IN ~~THE DREAM PORT~~ KOREA

ALL RIGHTS RESERVED. No part of this book can be reproduced or transmitted in any form or by any means without the permission of the copyright owner.

Dream It! Screw It! is an unlicensed, unauthorized parody with no association with The Walt Disney Company. Any pre-existing characters, theme parks, merchandise, attractions, and intellectual property referenced in this book are the sole property of The Walt Disney Company.

Dream It! Screw It! is a work of parody. All names and characters who appear in this parody are fictional and satirical representations. Any similarities to the creations in this book and living persons are purely coincidental. Also, don't sue us. We have no money!

"Succeeding is not really a life experience that does that much good. Failing is a much more sobering and enlightening experience."

–MICHAEL EISNER

INTRODUCTION

Like many pleasant, childlike men before me, I once pursued a career as an Imagineer for Walt Disney theme parks.

It's a highly competitive and sought after position. Only those who complete the Four Challenges of Goofy…

Decipher Walt's Ancient Riddle.

Design an attraction so perfect, only God could ride it.

Develop a strategy to "Imagineer" massive layoffs without alerting the press.

Defeat Golzor, the spike-wearing mutant, in hand-to-hand combat.

The author as a child in Disney World. His dreams of becoming an Imagineer would eventually "Wakka Wakka" away from him.

...may enter Disney's Great and Mighty Glendale Office, headquarters of Walt Disney Imagineering (WDI).

Years ago, I befriended a man at a comic book convention named Buddy Smiler. (That wasn't his real name, of course. His given name was Tad Winkler.) He worked at Imagineering for 25 years as a Disposal Copywriter. Buddy's job was to write the phrases put on trash cans around the park. He considered "Toss It, Friend!" to be his magnum opus. I was interested in meeting with Buddy to get his insight on how to break in at Imagineering, but he said he'd "do me one better."

He gave me box upon box of writing by an Imagineer named "Dipp," along with artwork drawn by staff artists to illustrate his proposals. Disney's powers-at-be attempted to throw these files away at one point, but Buddy –

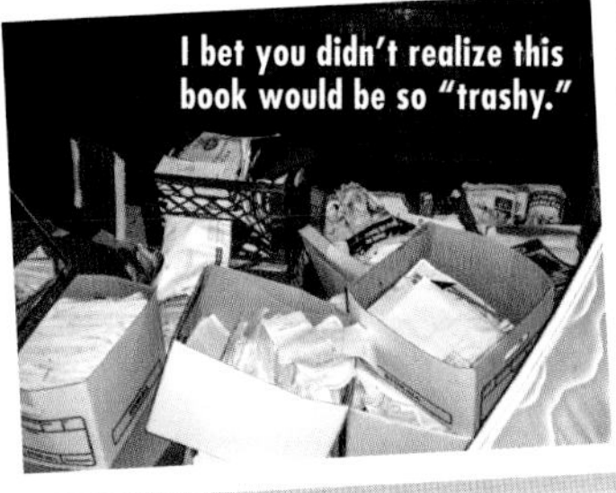
I bet you didn't realize this book would be so "trashy."

who was encouraged to take an obsessive interest in all things garbage — decided to rescue this lifetime of work from the cruel fate of Daisy Duck's Disposal Truck.

Dipp Disney was Walt Disney's cousin. He worked at Imagineering for 30 years, but he didn't become a household name like famous megastar Imagineers Zip Winkle, Martin O'Mallard or Larry Beans. So who exactly was he?

Buddy's files paint a portrait of an optimistic, energetic showman who kept on trying, no matter the odds. They also suggest Dipp was really, really stupid. And a drunk. And possibly a sex addict?

Supplementing Dipp's work is a "permanent record" of sorts, also rescued from the "Waste Please."There were copious notes taken about Dipp by another legendary Imagineer, Morton Dobbs. According to records, Morton was assigned – by Walt himself – to keep tabs on Dipp, and he never stopped, even after Walt's death. In fact, after Walt's death, Morton's notes increased twenty-fold!

When you drink upon a star...

"If you really want to understand Imagineering," Buddy advised, "study the life of Dipp Disney. Also, please take all this garbage. I can't live in trash anymore. I'm 87."

Through these documents, I pieced together the life and work of an unusual and forgotten artist. What you'll find in this volume is just the tip of the iceberg. As an official Creative Consultant at Imagineering, he generated 7000 theme park ideas, none of which were ever utilized. It's an incredible story, which I wanted to share with other fans of Disneyana, theme park design, and general sadness.

Some call him the worst Imagineer of all-time. Others counter that he was the best Imagineer, in that he was the best at coming up with the worst ideas. Most believe he's just a folk legend who never really existed. I believe there's some truth to all these opinions. Except the last one.

I hope you are ready, dear reader, for the incredible ride that was the life of Dipp Disney. There are more twists and turns than Space Mountain, with a story more preposterous than The Little Mermaid: Ariel's Undersea Adventure, and it's sure to make you queasier than the Tea Cups.

And so, I'm proud (?) to present the life and work of Mr. Dipp Disney...

There was one 'Country Bear' who did not like the Disney Boys.

DIPP'S EARLY YEARS

Walt Disney and his cousin Dipp grew up together in Marceline, Missouri. They were river playin' boys, skippin' stones and playin' with hobo bones.

One day in the woods, Walt grabbed a bear cub and made him dance for fun. Dipp saw the mama grizzly charge towards them and pushed Walt away, taking a bear swipe to the head. When Dipp awoke, he couldn't remember a thing. Walt told Dipp he tripped on a claw-shaped rock, so he wouldn't get in trouble. Dipp believed him, because the bear attack rendered him "stupid."

Walt moved to California to seek his fortune. Dipp stayed in Marceline and married his lifelong sweetheart, Cuddles (age 13), well past his prime (age 15). Dipp had many "careers": street fiddler, door-to-door galoshes polisher, ditch digger, ditch inspector, lab rat, ping pong ball mouth stuffer, kangaroo boxer. Dipp never had a job for more than a day. He preferred to whistle, drink, and tell stories than do the thing he was being paid to do.

Dipp couldn't provide for his family, and Cuddles had heard all his "Chinaman" jokes a thousand times. So his wife and 18 kids sent Dipp out to get them a pack of family cigarettes, knowing he'd get lost and never find his way back.

Dipp had two goals in life: 1. To make an impact on the world. Like his cousin Walt, he wanted to be recognized for making something spectacular. 2. Suck down as much moonshine as humanly possible.

In middle age, Dipp became homeless, destitute and dependent on alcohol. But through the hardships, Dipp never lost his signature smile, his love of whistling, or his "lucky" urine-soaked underwear.

His name helped him land a job scribbling Tijuana bibles for booze. One comic involved Mickey and Daisy having intercourse while Donald watched through a peephole. Dipp wondered what sort of children read these publications!

While investigating these illicit and illegal comics, Disney's lawyers discovered the existence of Dipp Disney.

"Should we rough him up 'til he changes his name?" one lawyer offered. "Put him out of his misery? Whatcha want us to do, Unca Walt?"

To their surprise, Walt asked them to bring Dipp to Burbank... *alive!*

Dipp's early work.

(1963-1966)

WALT GETS DIPPED OVER

When Walt heard about Dipp, living in a cardboard box and drawing Goofy's giant penis for moonshine, he was overcome with emotion. And that emotion was rage. What sort of person would besmirch the name and reputation of a defenseless, nonsensical man-dog?

But the more Walt thought about Dipp, the more his anger turned to guilt and remorse. After all, Dipp saved his life from an entirely unprovoked bear attack when they were just a couple of tree swingin' misfits. Now it was Dipp whose life needed saving. Walt stared thoughtfully at a bracelet on his arm that read, "What Would Gepetto Do?"

Meanwhile, Dipp arrived at Glendale and was immediately awestruck. Palm trees. Sunny skies. Cars zipped around on streets, instead of rusting tireless on lawns. The sign in front of the Baskin Robbins read "31 Flavors of Ice Cream," instead of "We Shoot Jews." What was this paradise, this... Glendale?

When Disney's legal team shoved Dipp into Walt's office, it was the first time they'd seen each other in 60 years. Walt sat Dipp down and told him wonderful stories about making movies, designing Disneyland, wanting to murder each and every one of those evil communist animators who went on strike, and creating magic for a living. Dipp told Walt a story about how he got his foot caught in a bear trap once, and after he was rescued by a forest ranger, got it caught in the same trap only 20 minutes later.

"Oh Dipp," Walt exclaimed. "You are full of stories, aren't you?"

So Walt offered Dipp "a job for life" at WED Enterprises (which would later be renamed Walt Disney Imagineering), the company that designed and developed Disneyland.

Upon seeing his cousin for the first time in half a decade, Walt was overcome with emotions (and horrible, horrible smells).

Morton Boggs: One "Sharp" Kid

Finally, this was Dipp's chance to make something spectacular. To create a legacy! And to live somewhere that didn't smell like wet garbage! Dipp was overjoyed.

"I've got pixie dust in my trousers, and I'm gonna sprinkle it all over this place," Dipp exclaimed and hugged Walt close.

"You need a shower," Walt replied.

Dipp was given an office, the title Creative Consultant and an assistant named Morton Boggs. Boggs had worked his way up from a shoe shine boy on Main Street to a shoe shine boy in Tomorrowland to Adventureland's Senior Shoe Shine Boy, and finally, Frontierland's President of Shineology and Shineography. Now he was Dipp's Assistant Pencil Sharpener.

"Listen closely, Morton," Walt instructed. "Dipp is a Disney, and as America knows, we Disneys are full of brilliant, marvelous ideas. As long as you work here, it will be your job to record everything Dipp says and does, so we don't lose any of his genius. Oh, and polish the roach carcass off the soles of the Oxfords in my office."

Morton took the job seriously. His loyalty, ambition, and analytical mind are what got him noticed for the Senior Shoe Shine Boy position. Now he was working inside WED Enterprises! Someday he hoped to run the place and become the Mayor of Disneyland. Of course, there was no such position, but he wouldn't let that stop him. Morton would let nothing stand in his way.

"I'm gonna stand in yer way, Mort-o" Dipp once told Morton. "I mean, I will stand in front of y'all, so y'all can push me, guide me to the meetin' room. I have had a bit too much Morning Moonshine." They didn't make it to that meeting.

Dipp's ideas for Disneyland attractions, which you'll read in the following pages, were not well-received by "the boys" at WED. They were often critiqued as "unsafe," "racist," and "WHAT?" As one of Dipp's colleagues put it during a presentation for what Dipp called "The Great Monorail Disaster," where every day a few randomly selected monorails would shake violently, as if they were about to crash, "Anything is possible in Disneyland, even ideas as hideous as this one."

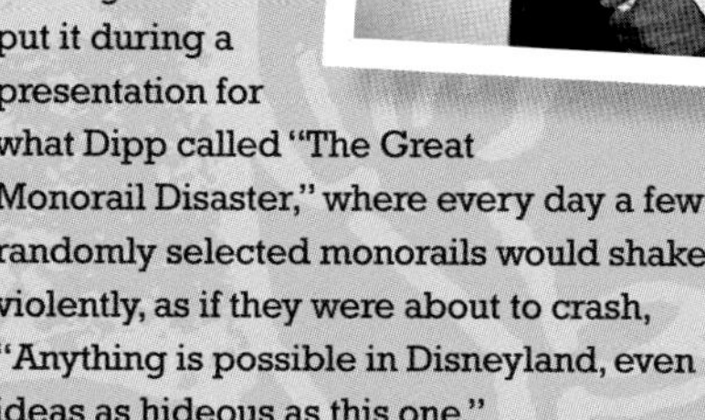

"No dream is off-limits here," Walt explained after another presentation, "except for the ones that involve gassing our guests. Do you understand?"

"I do now," Dipp nodded.

Walt was frustrated by the quality of Dipp's "notions." As far as ideas go, these weren't exactly $14 churros. However, Walt recognized that Dipp had plenty of enthusiasm and pluck, the precious qualities found in young, stupid, wonderful boys. Walt believed Dipp just needed more time to mature at WED and get into the swing of things.

Late in 1966, Walt passed away. Before he died, Walt put into writing that Dipp would have a job at Imagineering for the rest of his life. The paper contract was dipped in liquid iron, making it the first literal ironclad contract.

It's a Small World
(Child Feeding Zoo)

Year Developed: 1963
Intended Destination: 1964 New York World's Fair
Intended Sponsor: UNICEF
Original Assignment: Design a World's Fair pavilion for UNICEF, which provides emergency services and relief to underprivileged children around the world.

Attraction Summary: **Hungry children from around the world are brought to this fenced-in zoo. Guests step into UNICEF's shoes to feed and pet poor children first hand.**

Dippspiration: His very first job was at a petting zoo, where they had a food pellet dispenser. Dipp's job was to make sure guests didn't overfeed the animals. He failed, though Dipp did learn a valuable lesson: llamas can indeed get diabetes.

Walt encouraged Dipp to be forward thinking. So Dipp wondered if, rather than travel around the world, it wouldn't be more efficient for UNICEF to round up underprivileged youths and take them to their headquarters for feedings, vaccinations, and encouraging pats on the head. To create a "small world" for them.

Building Exterior: A dome painted green and blue ("colors of the world," Dipp explained). Along the sides of the dome are colorful, inspiring illustrations of adorable children holding their stomachs in pain.

Line Queue: As guests wait for their turn, they're treated to a catchy, cheerful song played over loud-speaker...

We can round them up
So they'll eat today
Take 'em from their homes
Feed 'em curds and whey

They would starve in their homes
Bring them all to our dome
It's a small world feeding zoo!

The Attraction: The feeding zoo itself is surrounded by a chain link fence. Inside, children are instructed to look sad until they are fed tomato slices, bread scraps, or cottage cheese from a vending machine. Mixed in with real children are lifelike dolls, happily bobbing their heads. "To balance out the sadness of the real children," Dipp explained.

Feedback: After Dipp presented this idea, Walt had many questions. Ever the stickler for details, Walt asked Dipp where the children would sleep. Dipp said he hadn't "imaginized" that far yet. And that was his answer for every one of Walt's follow-up questions.

Legendary Disney concept artist and porcelain doll collector Maureen Blue was often assigned to illustrate Dipp's work in the early years. Maureen didn't like the way Dipp stroked the hair on her dolls and called them "lil' angels." She said it made her dolls angry. (Note: The handwriting is Dipp's.)

Illustrator Maureen Blue was so unhappy with the way Dipp "tortured" her dolls, she drew the fish as dead in her concept art. Dipp assumed Maureen had drawn the fish "havin' themselves a lil' fish party."

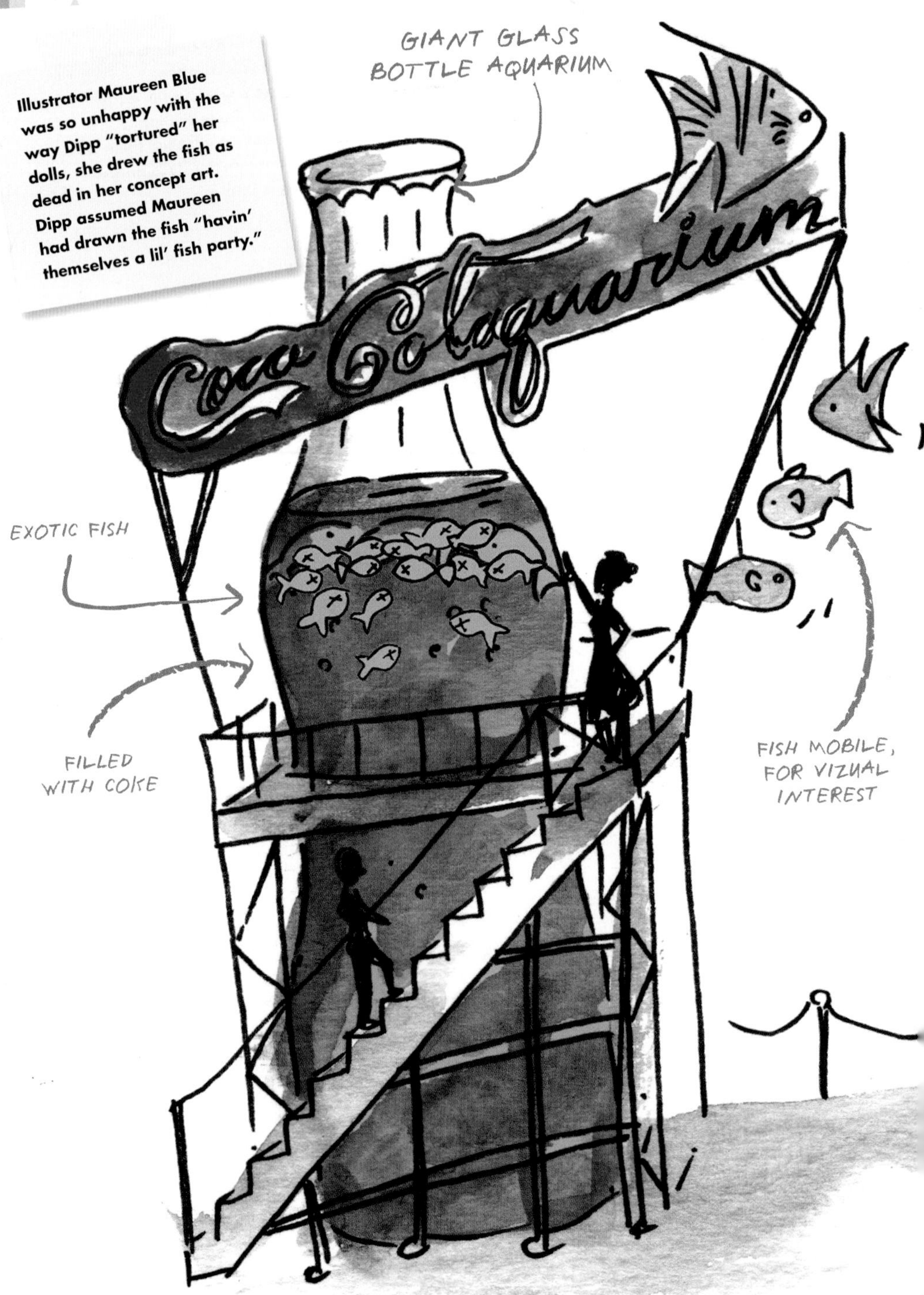

IDEA #06

Coca-Colaquarium

Year Developed: 1963
Intended Destination: 1964 New York World's Fair
Intended Sponsor: Coca-Cola
Original Assignment: Design a World's Fair pavilion for soda manufacturer Coca-Cola.

Attraction Summary: Real fish swim inside this giant glass bottle aquarium full of Coca-Cola, proving Coke is "the life force of the future."

Dippspiration: When Dipp was growing up, a bottle of Coke cost a nickel at the general store, while every other beverage – milk, orange juice, rubbing alcohol – cost 20-30 cents. To stretch their tight grocery budget, Dipp's poor, obese family only drank Coca-Cola.

So when Dipp found out Coca-Cola was interested in working with Disney for their pavilion, that got him thinking: "Maybe some day Coke will be cheaper than water, and that's all humans will ever drink!" But how would you demonstrate that Coke is as natural and healthy as "overrated" H2O?

The Attraction: A two-story fish tank shaped like a curvy glass Coke bottle, filled with bubbly Coca-Cola and exotic fish from around the world. A plaque on the side explains that in the future, humans will carbonate the oceans, and enjoy refreshing, all-natural Coca-Cola on tap, every day!

True Story: Ever the showman, Dipp pitched this idea to the team by presenting a bottle of Coca-Cola with a real fish floating inside. Morton worriedly pointed out that the fish was floating upside down at the very top of the bottle. Dipp assured the room that the fish was getting "a luxuriatin' massage by the gentle, refreshin', all-natural bubbles."

Feedback: Walt nixed this idea. According to his friends at Carnation, in 50 years poor families wouldn't drink soda at all, but rather, milk enhanced with muscle-building neutronium.

In the future, humans will carbonate the oceans...

The World's Biggest Number?!

Year Developed: 1963
Intended Destination: 1964 New York World's Fair
Intended Sponsor: IBM
Original Assignment: Design a World's Fair pavilion for leading computer developer IBM.

Attraction Summary: **Take a ride through the history of counting and perhaps you will discover... the world's biggest number!**

Dippspiration: Ten years ago, Dipp worked in a computer lab as a debugger. Granted, he was working as a cockroach "debugger," catching literal bugs by sticking his glue covered hands inside vacuum tubes. Still, he had touched computers, and "computers are the future, and they do math, and math is all about numbers, and numbers are good!" That was the intellectual foundation for this pitch.

Building Exterior: The building is mysteriously black with brightly colored numbers and question marks painted all over the walls. "422?" "97,566?" "-1?" The idea was to get people thinking about numbers, and more specifically, which one was the biggest. "Prime the number pump," Dipp explained.

Line Queue: As they wait, guests meet a friendly robot named Numbotron, which is either a man in a robot costume, "or preferably an acksual (sic) robo-man" with artificial intelligence. The friendly robot hands everyone in line a high tech punch card – to be used later!

The Attraction: Guests board their number canoe to voyage along the River of Math. They hear the vocoded, effeminate voice of Numbotron tell the story of counting.

In the first room, animatronic cavemen count the number of dinosaurs they killed that day. They use triceratops blood to write a line tally on the wall, but they can't count beyond four.

In the next room, bored animatrons of Thomas Jefferson and George Washington count the number of words in the Constitution and get to 4,543, "a very large number at the time."

In the third and final room, guests sail into the modern age, where animatronic scientists "tweak and tinker up" a giant computer terminal. Numbotron shrieks, "WHAT IS THE BIGGEST AND THEREFORE BEST NUMBER? WE MAY NEVER KNOW, BUT WE MUST KEEP TRYING. IT IS IMPORTANT."

Exit: As guests disembark, they put their punch cards into Numbotron and he prints out a custom number just for them. "Who knows?" Dipp smiled. "They might get... the biggest number."

Feedback: Walt patiently explained to Dipp that there was no "biggest number." After a long pause, Dipp replied with a slow wink.

ACKSHUAL ROBO-MAN
IMPRESSED BY ALL THIS MATH
HE SHOOTS OUT LOAD AFTER LOAD OF NUMBERS!

After drawing this, illustrator Maureen Blue asked Walt, "Speaking of numbers, how many more Dipp drawings will I have to do?" Walt reluctantly paid for one of her doll's "emergency hair surgery."

Illustrator Maureen Blue based the dog on her own beloved pup, Scruffles. Then Dipp asked her to completely redraw the dog and make him look "less sad and ugly," which resulted in the final version below. Maureen never spoke to Dipp again.

The Stinky Drinky Pirates

Year Developed: 1964
Intended Destination: New Orleans Square, Disneyland
Original Assignment: Reuse the successful boat ride mechanic from It's a Small World for a new ride themed around pirates.

Attraction Summary: **Yarr! Set sail for adventure and witness a crew of bloodthirsty pirates drink to forget the loved ones they left behind, who they miss very much.**

Dippspiration: Dipp had never been away from Missouri for so long, and was feeling a bit homesick. Also, now that he was earning a regular salary, all the booze he was drinking made him feel literally sick. One night, he puked in a garbage can that happened to be in an alley behind an AA meeting, and in that magical moment, he got Dippspired! (Not to seek help, but for a ride idea.)

Building Exterior: "Hispanish" saloon, 1850s.

Line Queue: Saloon walls are lined with framed portraits of scurvy pirates posing with treasure, skeletons, their patient wives and forlorn children. A barkeep hands out samples of "Pirate Fuel" (moonshine) to adults in line. Kids get a thimble of very strong cough syrup.

The Attraction: Guests board their pirate vessels and float into a dark room, where a floating skull warns them, "Dead men miss their wives!" The boat plummets down a waterfall, and guests soon realize their vessel is floating on Pirate Fuel! They can lean out the sides of their boat to scoop moonshine into their mouths.

Guests witness pirates invading a town! Well, "invading" in the sense that they're patronizing the town's fine bars and restaurants. These pirates need "a well-earned break from pirate activities" and want to knock back a few glasses of delicious Pirate Fuel in a relaxed setting.

The remaining rooms show one conversation that takes place between three pirates at a quiet bar. They discuss how they ache to see their families, how it's great to have friends they can really talk to, and about unearthing "buried treasure" (the emotions you bury deep down to be a successful pirate). They all sing a sea-shanty…

Yarr, Yarr! Yarr, Yarr!
We're pirates unwinding! (Yarr Yarr!)
We drink and relax, we cry and confess
Expressin' those feelings, yarr, yarr!
We all miss our families and struggle with stress
Don't suffer alone, y'all, yarr, yarr!
Yarr, Yarr! Yarr, Yarr!
We're pirates unwinding! (Yarr Yarr!)

True Story: Dipp once gave Walt a glass of "Pirate Fuel" from his private collection of toxic, semi-legal Missouri moonshine. After one quick swallow, Walt grabbed his throat in pain and screamed, "Are you trying to murder me?"

To which Dipp replied, "No sir, but those Stinky Drinky Pirates sure might!"

Instantation Transportation Station

Year Developed: 1966
Intended Destination: Tomorrowland, Disneyland
Original Assignment: Design new attractions to give Tomorrowland a major facelift, with a focus on the future of transportation.

Attraction Summary: **In the future, you will travel anywhere in seconds. Experience teleportation with this magical, chemically-produced simulation.**

Dippspiration: A spaceship could go 17,500 miles per hour, but Dipp claimed to have personally experienced what he called "instantational transportisment" (teleportation).

Building Exterior: An all-white, angular bus stop. "By 1999, this will replace the bus! Look out buses, here comes us-es!" Dipp promised.

Line Queue: There are all-white benches for sitting and an all-white snack machine, serving all-white bags of "white flavored" Ruffles.

The Attraction: One at a time, guests are ushered into glass tubes, called TelePods. (A combination of "teleportation" and "pods," Dipp carefully explained.) Suddenly, lights flicker! The TeleAir (teleportation air) fogs up around the guest.

Exit: Next thing they know, guests find themselves in the all-white dumpster in the all-white alley behind Instantation Transportation Station!

Feedback: After a presentation to a group of Imagineers, Walt was intrigued. He wanted to know how it worked. "Simple," Dipp explained. "There was this one time a man put a rag on my face–"

"Chloroform!" an Imagineer shouted. The Imagineers immediately began exchanging money. It seems a few of the boys placed bets on how Dipp's transportation of the future worked.

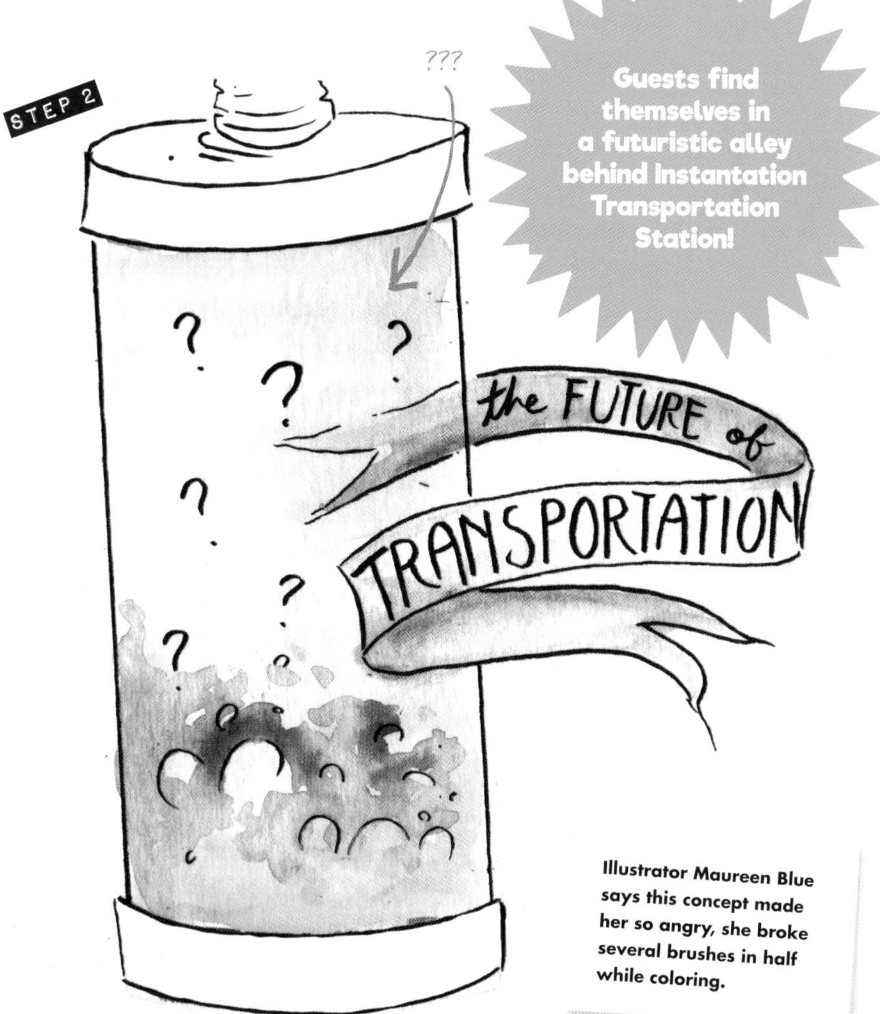

Guests find themselves in a futuristic alley behind Instantation Transportation Station!

Illustrator Maureen Blue says this concept made her so angry, she broke several brushes in half while coloring.

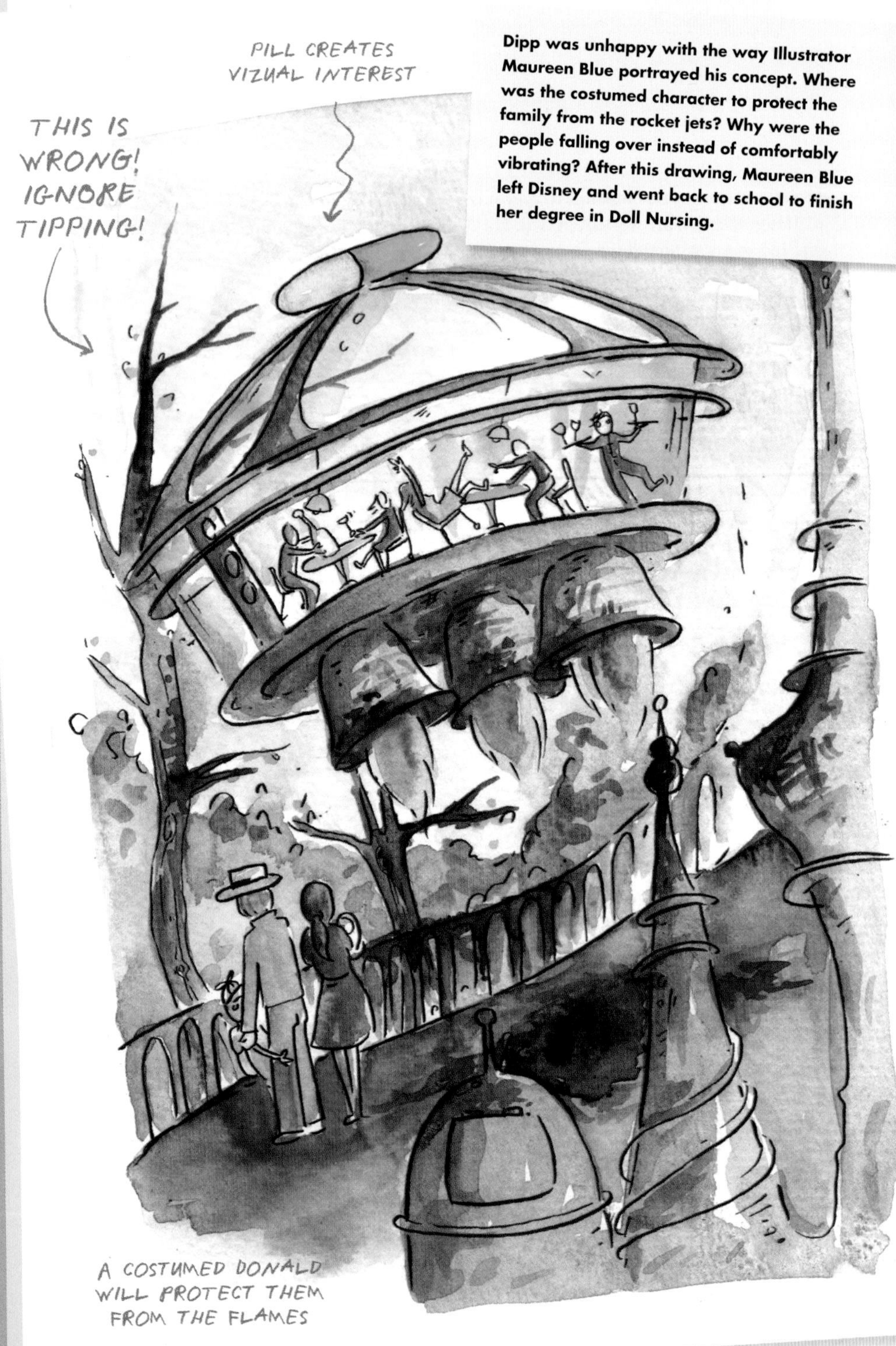

Dipp was unhappy with the way Illustrator Maureen Blue portrayed his concept. Where was the costumed character to protect the family from the rocket jets? Why were the people falling over instead of comfortably vibrating? After this drawing, Maureen Blue left Disney and went back to school to finish her degree in Doll Nursing.

The Hoverstaurant

Year Developed: 1966
Intended Destination: Tomorrowland, Disneyland
Original Assignment: Design new attractions to give Tomorrowland a major facelift, with a focus on the future of transportation.

Attraction Summary: Rotating restaurants are a thing of the past. This full-service sit down restaurant hovers around Tomorrowland on jets and serves food of the future, like chicken pills!

Dippspiration: When Dipp was homeless, he once snuck into a rotating restaurant to try and steal a slice of boysenberry pie. He was caught when the circular rotation made him so dizzy, he projectile vomited for 30 minutes in a circular pattern across the floor of the kitchen.

Opening Thoughts: "For too long, man has been forced to make the ultimate choice: cutting edge transportation or fine dinin'. Ya can't eat a steak on a monorail, they'll throw ya right off! And when ya order a steak at a fancy restaurant, the table ain't moving nowhere." –Dipp Disney

Building Exterior: A circular, copper 4500 square foot spacecraft constantly floating in the air via rocket jets. Imagine a cutting edge kitchen appliance from the 1900s that is the size of a building and floating around. The Hoverstaurant travels around Tomorrowland 20 feet in the air. To ensure the safety of passersby, costumed characters march alongside the restaurant, intercepting children with hugs to prevent them from touching the jet flames.

The Attraction: Inside, guests find a dazzling mix of lights on strings and a black carpet with a star pattern. "Dinin' guests will feel like they're floatin' in space," Dipp explains. "Like an astronaut, or me after enough moonshine!" Your plastic "astro-chair" has a safety belt, just in case "the restaurant experiences any turbularies (sic)."

The menu theme: "Light" Foods. The menu includes Saturnian Salad (a cobb salad with a ring of tuna), fruit salad (grapes and cantaloupe slices), and the star attraction? A wide assortment of meal pills: artificially flavored protein powder capsules. The pills Dipp pitched included "Mickey's Meatloaf Meteor" and "Chicken of the Space."

Feedback: Here are a few notes Dipp received from fellow Imagineers:

"The walkways of Tomorrowland aren't wide enough to accommodate a flying restaurant."

"There's a real danger that surrounding buildings and guests could catch on fire from the restaurant's rocket jets."

"These pills taste disgusting. Who gave you these pills?"

NULL AND ROY'D!

The death of Walt Disney sent shockwaves through WED Enterprises. A close relative of Walt's would have to step in and take the helm at Disney Imagineering. It would obviously not be Dipp.

Roy Disney was Walt's practical and pragmatic older brother. He was a co-founder of Disney and ran the business side of things, while Walt oversaw costly box office flops like *Fantasia* and *Pinocchio*. In Roy's mind, the real magic of Disney was "magically" keeping the company's books balanced.

In 1966, Roy Disney delayed his retirement to oversee the elaborate "Florida Project," which he eventually named Walt Disney World, in honor of his brother. One family member who Roy had no intention of honoring was Dipp Disney. Growing up, he openly referred to Dipp as "my idiot cousin" to family, a nickname which quickly spread throughout the state of Missouri.

Dipp became known as The Phantom of the Office.

Whereas Roy was firm and fair, Dipp was loosy *and* goosey. To Roy, Dipp's ideas were always costly, ill-conceived and at times made him very uncomfortable. (See Pluto's Retreat, p. 26.) Roy thought Dipp was dead weight, an unnecessary and aggrevating expense on the balance sheet.

Unfortunately for Roy, Walt hiring Dipp *ad infinitum* was a unilateral decision. So now Roy had to deal with a drunk, happy-go-lucky roadblock, slowing down project meetings with terrible ideas, like a gator wrestling pit in the middle of Adventureland. ("Why not take advantage of Florida's natural wonders?" Dipp said.)

Roy tired to figure out how to forcibly retire his troublesome cousin. He banished Dipp to the sidelines of WED, moving him from a corner office with a window to an unused utility closet in the basement. He never put Dipp on projects, and encouraged the other Imagineers to look away from Dipp at the cafeteria. Maybe if everyone ignored Dipp, he would simply vanish.

Dipp thought everyone was playing a joke on him. A years long practical joke. To his credit, even though the lack

Roy's plan failed.

of human contact made him a little crazy and gave him an eye twitch, he kept on whistling and smiling. Whistling and smiling. For years, the janitorial staff were convinced Dipp was a chubby, whistling ghost.

Meanwhile, Roy took a liking to Morton, who was known around the office for having "the creepiest laugh," but was also practical and hard-working. He became Roy's assistant, and encouraged Morton to unlearn everything he learned from shadowing Dipp, like how to pick your toes with a rubber hose, and that was pretty much it. In late 1971, Morton was promoted to full-fledged Imagineer. Roy promised to mentor him, saying "we'll be spending a lot of time together."

Roy died the next day. He was taking welding workshops, so he could personally melt Dipp's contract and fire his cousin once and for all. The job of what to do with Dipp would soon fall to his protégé, Morton, who later came up with a "creative" solution.

Some believe Dipp was the cause of Roy's death. Here is the transcript from Roy's last meeting at WED, so you can judge for yourself. Roy was giving Dipp "constructive feedback" on his proposal for the Florida version of Mr. Toad's Wild Ride. Dipp wanted to eliminate the tracks, give the guests free liquor, and allow them to slam their vehicles head first into prop trees, buildings, and Badger. He thought it'd be fun to give guests "the true Mr. Toad drinkin' and drivin' experience."

"Do you really think this is a sharp *notion*, Dipp?" Roy yelled, spitting with anger. "Encouraging riders to get drunk and recklessly operate vehicles on Disney property? And why do so many of your ideas involve giving free liquor to guests? *There will never, ever be alcohol served in Disney parks.* Get that through your thick skull. I don't know what my brother saw in you, idiot, but this charade has gone on long enough. The Imagineers are highly educated and skilled individuals at the tops of their professions. You have no training, no usable life experience, no aptitude – the only things you're good at are drinking and whistling, but there are currently no vacancies in the Country Bears Jamboree–!" Roy coughed furiously, then grabbed his chest in pain. A secretary tried to help him, but he waved her off. "You should do the decent thing and quit, Dipp. I was trying to give you a hint by ignoring you for years, but you're so stupid, you... you... and stop abusing company hoses–"

At which point, Roy collapsed on the floor and was ushered to the hospital. Dipp was sad when Roy passed. During his eulogy for his cousin, Dipp described their relationship as one built on "mutual respect."

Hindenburg Sky Resort

Year Developed: 1968
Intended Destination: Walt Disney World
Original Assignment: Concept ideas for Walt Disney World's first hotels (even though the Contemporary Resort and Polynesian Resort were already being built).

Attraction Summary: **What if the Hindenburg never crashed? It would have become this flying luxury hotel in the clouds, casting a dark shadow over Disney's newest park.**

Dippspiration: Dipp was fascinated by the Hindenburg crash. He was a self-described "Hindenberg truther," who believed "the fire was a conspiracary (sic) enacted by the Illuminatary (sic), in combination with God, to prevent humans from gettin' too close to the Pearly Gates."

Building Description: The hotel is a replica of the original LZ 129 Hindenburg blimp with magical Disney touches. Like the original, there's a music salon with a map of the world on the wall – only now it's a map of *Disney World*. Guests enjoy world class dining with a menu of the finest "light" foods, like filet mignon pills (Dipp would not give up on food pills). And unlike the original Hindenburg, instead of performing propaganda missions for Hitler and the Nazi party, "it will *not* do that."

Special Events: Every evening at 7 pm, fake fires go off in the lobby. Announcements ask that everyone remain calm, but guests can feel the resort plunging and losing altitude. As the fires continue to burn, the announcements get more grim, admitting that a crash is highly likely, and asking passengers to pray to Jesus Christ for forgiveness.

At this point, the guests are panicking. Children are crying. Cast members attempting to fight the "fire" suddenly "catch fire" themselves, and run around the hotel screaming their heads off! (In his presentation, Dipp tried to set fire to the drapes in Roy's office, but Roy wrestled away his lighter.)

Before the resort crashes to the ground in a fiery explosion, we hear an announcement in a thick German accent: "Das anyvon know how to fly de exploding blimp?" Then we hear a familiar, high pitched voice. "A-ha! I'll give it a shot! Captain Mickey to the rescue," at which point the resort regains altitude and zips back up to the sky. It was all just a bit of Disney horseplay!

Proposed Slogan: "Oh, the Amenities!™"

Feedback: After the meeting, Dipp asked Roy if he'd ever heard of a disaster on the scale of the Hindenburg. Roy joked, "I have. Your career in Imagineering." Dipp didn't get it.

Legendary animator Nick Javits was one of Walt's original "Nine Ancients." When no one else would acknowledge Dipp's existence, Nick agreed to illustrate his concepts, in exchange for "an ol' fashioned Missouri hand rub." Nick loved getting rubs.

THIS IS GONNA BE ONE
SLOPPY SYMPHONY!

Animator Nick Javits insisted Dipp give him a very special rub to render this illustration. (A foot rub.) (Followed by a handjob.)

Pluto's Retreat

Year Developed: 1968
Intended Destination: Walt Disney World
Original Assignment: Concept ideas for Walt Disney World hotels (even though the Contemporary Resort and Polynesian Resort were already being built).

Attraction Summary: **Get into the swing of things! This hotel is for "free lovin'" couples who wish to experience "unparalleled ecstasy" with a little help from Pluto, Mickey and the gang.**

Dippspiration: During his months long isolation from Roy and the other Imagineers, Dipp decided to return to his Tijuana bible roots and poorly drew a 200 page graphic novel sex odyssey entitled *Fannytasia*, which collected comics like "The Buttcracker Suite," "Night in Bald Mountains," and "Mickey Puts His Mouse Penis Inside a Magical Hat." The project naturally led him to this hotel idea.

Building Description: The hotel's aesthetic was described as "ancient Rome meets a lot of velvet," with marble pillars, velvet love seats, and enlarged versions of his own *Fannytasia* artwork on display in gold-leaf frames. Highlights of Pluto's Retreat include The Jungle Baths, where guests "take off their loincloths and go feral," Skinderella's Cinema, a porn theatre screening classic XXX Disney parodies like *Humpy the Love Butt*, and a breakfast buffet with new mascot character Linda Ducklace, who offers to "deep quack" men after they finish their fruit salads (grapes and cantaloupe slices).

The main attraction? Pluto's Playroom, a 24/7 masked orgy where all participants are given costume heads of Mickey, Minnie, Donald – the whole gang (bang)! Get into double trouble with Chip 'n' Dale and let Pinocchio "lie" inside you. It's a once in a lifetime "sex-perience."

Special Events: Upon arrival, couples each receive a room key. Everyone drops their keys into a crystal bucket, then each guest "lets their questin' fingers" pick out a different key for "an orgasmic arrival!" As you pick, a 1930's "Barber-Schtupp Quartet" in the lobby sings you "The Key Picking Song"...

Pull out a key
For a scandalous trip!
You might get Sam or Suzy
Or a nice man named Dipp!

(Dipp's key is always present in the bowl.)

Proposed Slogan: "Free Love – Doggy Style!"

Feedback: Dipp proposed this idea to Roy while he was in the restroom. Roy asked to see his work, then threw all the artwork and notes into the closest toilet. The toilet was so clogged it wouldn't flush (lucky for us!). Dipp fished out his materials and blow-dried them.

The Haunted Mansons

Year Developed: 1970
Intended Destination: Liberty Square, Magic Kingdom
Original Assignment: Build a larger version of the successful Haunted Mansion attraction in Florida. (Note: Dipp was not chosen for the design team, but that didn't stop him from pitching this.)

Attraction Summary: **Charles Manson and his murderous cultists take up residence in a new wing of the Florida version of Disney's haunted house.**

Dippspiration: During this time, Dipp was undergoing a "disquieting metamorphosis." He had endured two years of being ignored by Roy and most of his colleagues, which made him jittery, nervous and paranoid. After all, what's a showman without an audience? During his free time, which was all the time, Dipp was reading story after story about a series of terrifying murders...

Room Description: Dipp described the proposed scene for this classic dark ride with a Paul Frees-esque narration: "Our tour continues with Polanski's Parlor, where these freaky hippies are having a 'killer' time. There's master manipulator Charlie Manson in the corner, singing into a... 'squeal-to-squeal' tape deck. Which type of spooks will survive his phantom race war? Listen closely to his tune of doom...

[To the tune of "Surfin' U.S.A."]
When the black panther monsters rise up
Incited by what we say
The white skeletons will crumble
Helter Skelter - Yay!

Oh no! It's 'curtains' for this popular movie actress, who's being cut out of our freaky film. They claim The Beatles are 'very cool' with this..."

True Story: Dipp hid in the utility closet of a meeting room for a full day, so he could surprise the Haunted Mansion team. He lept out wearing a fake gray beard, a plastic butcher knife and a big "X" drawn on his forehead. He screamed, "Greetings, all y'all PIGGIES!"

Roy grabbed his chest, forcing himself to not have a heart attack. "Don't let the idiot get to you," Roy muttered to himself.

Feedback: Roy tried to throw Dipp out a window, but was eventually subdued.

Animator Nick Javits, who created this concept illustration, was the first to tell Dipp about the Mansons while receiving his "daily rub." Before he died, Javits confessed that was "not a good idea."

After completing this illustration, and getting a final full body rub from Dipp, animator Nick Javits officially resigned from Imagineering. "You have a lot of magic in you," Nick wrote to Dipp. "Not so much in your head, but definitely in your hands. Wowza!"

The Water and Electrical Appliances Parade

Year Developed: 1971
Intended Destination: Rivers of America, Disneyland
Intended Sponsor: General Electric
Original Assignment: Concept new nighttime parades for Disneyland.

Attraction Summary: **In this spectacular floating parade, giant toasters and hairdryers plunge into the lake, causing surges of electricity to light up the night sky!**

Dippspiration: Dipp theorized the reason why Disney World's Electrical Water Pageant resonated with guests: they were anticipating major sparks if an electric float accidentally sank into the Seven Seas Lagoon. He cited the gasps from audiences to a scene in *Goldfinger* where James Bond smacks an electric fan at a bad guy in a bathtub, shocking him to death in a beautiful red glow. "I wanna give guests that 'Am I gonna die now?' excitement they crave."

Parade Theme: Imagine giant toasters, hairdryers, microwaves, TV sets and popcorn poppers all fully charged, floating on platforms. The glow of the microwave and the blinking 12:00 of a digital alarm clock illuminating the night sky.

When the platforms submerge, the appliances plunge into the water, and they light up the lagoon with spectacular currents. The last float is the three speed record changer and stereo system the parade's soundtrack is playing on. As it sinks, the stereo creates a mix of crackling audio and crackling, deadly electricity flowing through the lake.

Feedback: In order to make this presentation in front his colleagues, Dipp had to temporarily lock Roy in a utility closet. Roy was so upset, he eventually punched his way through the wooden closet door. Keep in mind that he was 78 at the time.

One Imagineer pointed out that putting an appliance in a bathtub doesn't actually make the water glow or spark at all. Another asked how they could afford to replace water damaged 20 ft. tall appliances every night. Dipp answered both queries with the words "pixie dust," followed by his signature slow wink.

"I wanna give guests that 'Am I gonna die now?' excitement they crave."

HO CHI DIPP

Before Roy Disney passed away, he named his Imagineering protégé – Morton "Morton" Boggs – as his successor. He was given the title Chief Creative Executive, but insisted everyone call him "Mayor." Finally, Morton had arrived.

Morton was not fun. He thought guests should have fun, and Imagineers should work. Constantly. This was in direct contrast with Dipp, a self-proclaimed "goof about town" who spent his days "working" on a cornjug of moonshine.

Morton wanted to begin his term as "Mayor" by finishing the job his mentor could not – getting rid of Dipp Disney. He remembered a story Dipp told him: Dipp never saw his family after getting lost trying to buy a pack of cigarettes. So, one day, Morton called Dipp into his office. Dipp was being sent on a "top secret special assignment" to get new ideas for Adventureland by exploring the tropics of Vietnam. (If Dipp couldn't find his way back from a corner store, how would he ever make it back from Vietnam?) Dipp was honored to be entrusted with a special assignment of any kind, and fortunately for Morton, he was absurdly uninformed about current events.

Imagineers would snicker when Morton wore the sash. He reminded them of Mayor McCheese.

Now a top executive, Morton had access to the secret Disney jet, Air Force Fun. He paid a mafia "jet guy" to discreetly fly Dipp to South Vietnam and abandon him there. On the plane ride over, Dipp felt very special and appreciated. "I'm going to Vietnog!" Dipp crowed while chugging his special "bug juice" (moonshine with a secret ingredient: bee carcasses).

He was abandoned and left to wander the jungle aimlessly. Dipp thought back to a training film he saw about getting lost in nature, *Snow White and the Seven Dwarves*, and tried whistling for helpful critters. Instead he drew the attention of

Dipp on his way to the plane. He thought 'Vietnog' was a Hawaiian island.

the Viet Cong, who were not very helpful. In fact, they kidnapped Dipp and placed him in a POW camp. ("Very un-critter-like," Dipp would later recall.) Conditions in the camp were brutal, but Dipp never stopped whistling a happy tune, despite being imprisoned in a bamboo cage, where his fellow captives screamed at him to "stop all that goddamn whistling!"

Dipp revealed who he was to his captors. The young Viet Cong soldiers got very excited. They heard stories about Disneyland, and dreamed of the day they could overthrow that imperialist warlord Mickey Mouse and take over his bourgeois kingdom of amusements for the working class.

The soldiers put Dipp to work designing and building a Disneyland attraction of their own, at gunpoint. Dipp created a variation on a Disney classic, which he called The Enchanted Cù Chi Room (next page).

The attraction Dipp designed – ornery birds let loose inside a hut – surprised the soldier in attendance, who opened fire on the birds. The ensuing chaos created a distraction allowing American prisoners to escape, taking Dipp with them.

In Glendale, Disney lawyers heard the rumor that a bootleg Disneyland was being built in communist Vietnam. They planned a stealth mission to investigate. The lawyers found and rescued Dipp, who got lost in the jungle when the freed POWs asked him to fetch a pack of cigarettes.

Dipp returned to WED Enterprises in 1975 with the Presidential Medal of Freedom. President Gerald Ford called Dipp a "national hero and brilliant military strategist." According to Dipp's contract, if he ever won a Presidential accomodation, he was to be given a 20% pay raise.

At Morton's behest, Dipp never mentioned he was there for Morton's "special assignment." Morton told Dipp he didn't want to take any credit (or legal responsibility) for his bravery.

Dipp's story was later adapted into a feature film, *Rambo: First Blood*.

Ford allegedly asked Dipp to turn the Lincoln Bedroom into an Enchanted Cu Chi Room, "but with no murderous birds."

IDEA #783

THE ENCHANTED CỦ CHI ROOM

Year Developed: 1971-75
Intended Destination: POW Camp, South Vietnam
Original Assignment: Build a Disneyland attraction or die.

Attraction Summary: **A flock of wild jungle birds "wing it" and put on an unforgettable musical show!**

Dippspiration: Dipp did not want to die. However, he had no practical experience building anything. His one day on the job as a construction worker ended when a nearly completed three story office building collapsed into rubble after Dipp "goofed up" with a wrecking ball. (His job was to chase away squirrels entering the construction site.) However, not wanting to die is a very good motivator.

Behind the Scenes: Dipp was given the largest hut in the village to build inside. He spent years carving and painting homemade tiki masks, and with the help of a few young villagers, captured and caged many jungle birds. Dipp purposefully under-fed the birds, thinking it would motivate them to work harder on stage. It only made the birds very, very enraged.

The Attraction: After years of building and fine tuning, Dipp was ready to unveil his creation. First, the soldiers were required to wait in an absurdly long line for pineapple juice. When the soldiers were seated with their juice cups, Dipp began singing a chirpy, repetitive tune…

In The Củ Chi Củ Chi Củ Chi Củ Chi
Củ Chi Room
In The Củ Chi Củ Chi Củ Chi Củ Chi
Củ Chi Room
When the birds are unfurled
You'll applaud and swoon!
In The Củ Chi Củ Chi Củ Chi Củ Chi
Củ Chi Room

He opened the bird cage, but the jungle birds wouldn't come out at first. They stood motionless, staring. According to Dipp, they had "stage jitters," so he violently rattled the cage, forcing his flock of malnourished performers into the enclosed hut.

Feedback: The soldiers screamed as a giant flock of frightened birds were released all at once. They pecked at the soldiers, who shot at the birds with machine guns. It's fair to say the show didn't go exactly as Dipp had imagineered.

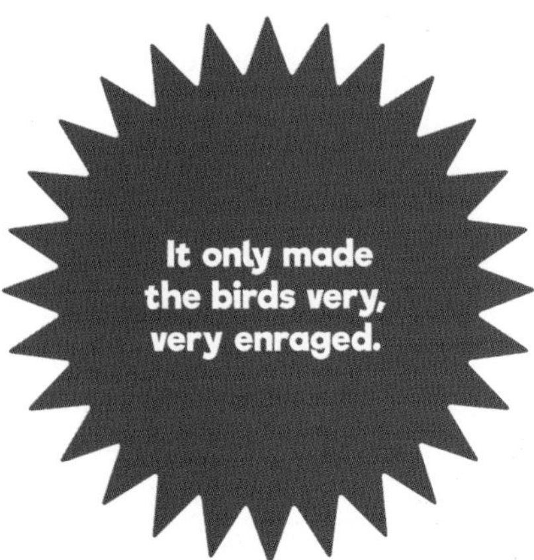
It only made the birds very, very enraged.

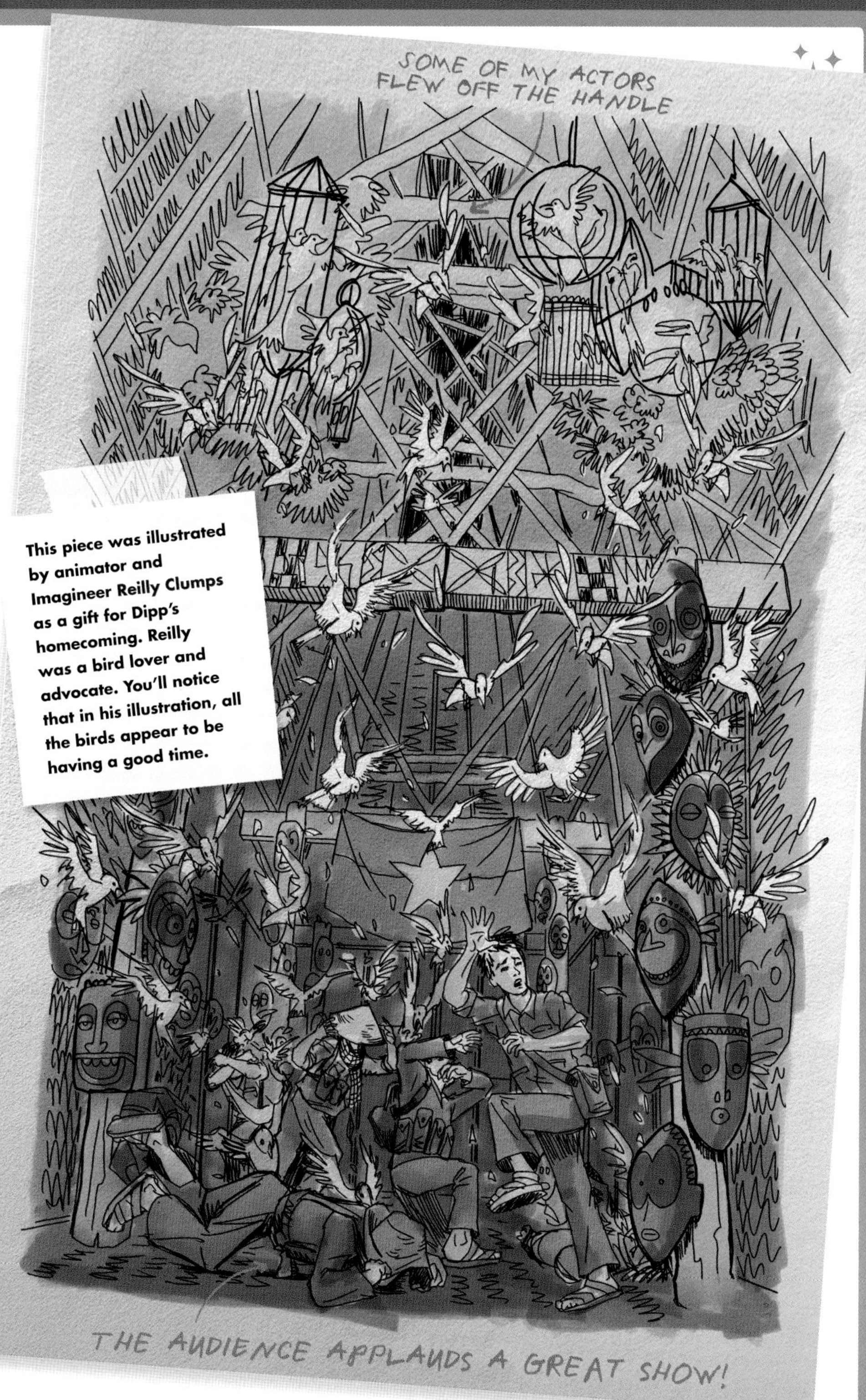

SOME OF MY ACTORS FLEW OFF THE HANDLE
THE AUDIENCE APPLAUDS A GREAT SHOW!

This piece was illustrated by animator and Imagineer Reilly Clumps as a gift for Dipp's homecoming. Reilly was a bird lover and advocate. You'll notice that in his illustration, all the birds appear to be having a good time.

(1975-1984)

SPACE DIPP EARTH

Walt Disney's original vision for the Florida Project included a futuristic city called EPCOT, the Experimental Prototype Community of Tomorrow. After Walt passed, The Walt Disney Company decided not to move forward with Walt's vision for a modern urban utopia, and instead focused on creating a working version of Flubber, so *Flubber* movies would cost less to produce.

However, while Dipp was using untrained birds to maim and entertain overseas, a cult of Imagineers at WED decided to keep Walt's dream for EPCOT alive. They proposed the creation of a theme park representing the ideals of EPCOT, a concept that made Disney's lawyers a lot less nervous than an actual city with real, non-animatronic people living inside it.

Originally, Spaceship Earth was designed to be the world's most advanced, high tech gift shop.

Why did Morton put Dipp on the design team? After getting interrogated by the FBI for weeks regarding his "unusual" use of a Disney aircraft, Morton wanted to make sure his relationship with war hero Dipp was cordial.

MORTON BOGGS' PYRAMID OF
IMAGINEERING SUCCESSGINEERING
All you need to know about Imagineering in one chart.
A Prayer to Walt's Ghost
Fluffing
Build an Entire Attraction
Visual Overloading
Spirit Quest for Sponsorship
Bad Idea Filtration
Blue Sky Story Dream-Catching

In Dipp's absence, Morton became the creative and administrative lead at Imagineering. He named and formalized seven stages of the ideation process, along with hundreds of sub-stages. The early project meetings to discuss ideas were called "Blue Sky" meetings, and his formal policy was that no critique or judgement

Dipp and Morton, two not friends.

would be made in a Blue Sky meeting. All ideas were welcome. His superiors praised Morton's instinct to segment and micromanage the creative process, calling it "very Walt-like."

This policy for Blue Sky meetings, that no idea was shot down, came back to bite "Mayor" Morton in the sash. Now he had to endure Dipp's many terrible ideas for EPCOT (like a motion simulator depicting a journey to heaven called the Wonders of Death) and find positive things to say about them.

Ultimately, tension built to unmanagable levels between Morton and Dipp. Morton could no longer pretend Dipp's ideas were not horrible, and Dipp became frustrated that his notions – now receiving scant praise! – were still not being realized in the parks.

Dipp was always fond of moonshine, but he began to depend on it again, like he had back in his "drawin' dirty Donald doinkin' Daisy" days. He was discouraged and wondered if he would ever succeed in his quest to make a mark on the world. All his "markings," his hundreds of ideas, went into a filing cabinet, and more than once, those filing cabinets were thrown into incinerators.

Dipp's drinking did not go unnoticed by Morton, who had just discovered a loophole in Dipp's ironclad contract. If Dipp was unable to physically perform his duties as an Imagineer, he could be dismissed. For example, if Dipp was comatose for years, or perhaps in a days-long drinking stupor...

After a long drought of assignments, Morton finally put Dipp on a team developing an E-Ticket attraction for Critter Country. (See "Moonshine Mountain," p. 48.) Dipp decided to "research" the South by drinking more of his authentic, mouth numbing moonshine than ever, which Morton encouraged. "Good luck with that research," Morton sneered.

Dipp couldn't walk straight for a month. Whenever his colleagues brought this up, or suggested AA, Dipp whistled as loud as he could, with a big grin on his face.

Finally, during his presentation for Moonshine Mountain, Dipp passed out onto the floor and created an unpleasant smelling "waterfall" in his pants, trickling down his legs.

That was all the ammunition Morton needed to fire him. He came into work the next day beaming, filled-out pink slip in hand, when he learned of a sudden and important change in management...

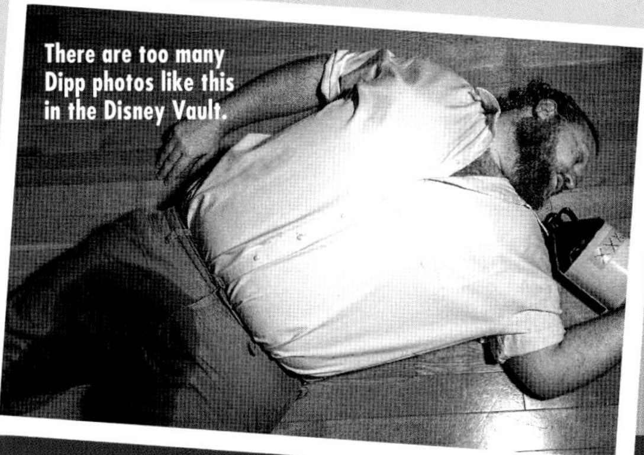
There are too many Dipp photos like this in the Disney Vault.

VIETNAMESE JUNGLE CRUISE

Year Developed: 1975
Intended Destination: South Vietnam Pavilion in World Showcase, EPCOT Center
Intended Sponsor: The Provisional Revolutionary Government of the Republic of South Vietnam
Original Assignment: Create pavilion ideas for World Showcase – a section of EPCOT Center with a series of side-by-side pavilions themed around countries of the world, a model for peace.

Attraction Summary: Come face-to-face with wild tigers, unpredictable birds, and gorillas – or rather, *guerillas,* in this boat tour through the dangerous jungles of South 'Nam.

Dippspiration: In Dipp's words: "I saw some crazy poop in 'Nam, y'all. Villages burned to the ground. Innocents slaughtered in the road. Soldiers blown apart limb by limb. And the only thing I could think, while I was bein' held hostage all those years in that godforsaken place… was how do we bring this incredible adventure to Walt Disney World?!"

Pavilion Theme: The pavilion looks like a tiny village inside a dangerous, blood-soaked jungle. It features spiked trapdoor activity rooms for kids, and a noodle shack called Phở Chi Minh, where guests are served "traditional, flavorless glook (sic) food" by "the kind of shy ladies y'all see there."

The centerpiece of the pavilion is the Vietnamese Jungle Cruise, a wildlife boat adventure! The story of the ride is that you thought you were traveling through the canals of Vienna, but accidentally booked a trip to Vietnam. "Countries with 'V' names are easily mixed-up!"

Line Queue: Guests cut their own path through thick jungle foliage using machetes (sold at a nearby kiosk), then wade waist-deep into a muddy stream. The boat captain, your tour guide, lifts guests into the boat. Overweight guests are "sadly left behind."

The Attraction: On the ride, guests encounter animatronic wildlife, which serves as fodder for the tour guide's corny jokes. (ex. When passing a leopard: "Cat got your fun?") All of a sudden, their affable guide is slaughtered by Viet Cong soldiers! Their ship is hijacked and now enroute to a POW camp underneath a manmade waterfall.

And who should come to guest's rescue? It's brave US soldiers Sgt. Mickey, Pvt. Goofy, and Baloo the Mercenary, all packing M-60 rifles. They fire at your boat, accidentally slaughtering a few civilians on board (played by Vietnamese cast members), but in the end they take control of your boat and get you out of this quagmire "y'all got yourself into in the first place."

Feedback: "Well, I can say this. It builds on a pre-existing ride structure, which is cost effective." –Morton

REAL FACE OF DEATH! CAST WILL STUDY FOOTAGE OF DYING SOLDIERS

FAKE BB GUNS

In this era of his "career," Dipp was often paired with Harv Ritzman, the most senior Imagineer. Harv is best known for drawing the first official illustration of a man being run down by a Disneyland parade float for a now discontinued safety brochure. He was a bit of a sadist.

There's only one thing Imagineer Harv Ritzman enjoyed drawing more than people getting gunned down, and that's people starving to death. "This was a real hoot," Harv said about working on this illustration.

COMMUNISM: HOW GREAT IS IT, ANYWAY?

Year Developed: 1975
Intended Destination: Soviet Union Pavilion in World Showcase, EPCOT Center
Intended Sponsor: The Union of Soviet Socialist Republics
Original Assignment: Create pavilion ideas for World Showcase – a section of EPCOT Center with a series of side-by-side pavilions themed around countries of the world, a model for peace.

Attraction Summary: Witness the splendor and superiority of Russian communism in a glorious 360 degree Circlevision film.

Dippspiration: In Dipp's words: "I think everybody here would agree that Communism is the future. After all, my former captors, and the most honorable Tôn Đức Thắng, winner of the Stalin Peace Prize, are all in agreement on that there point. My question is this: How're we gonna bring Communism to the fat bourgeois tourist pigs visiting EPCOT?"

Pavilion Theme: Red Square, Moscow. Communist soldiers march in lockstep through the streets. Costumed character versions of Marx and Lenin perform a musical stage show called *The Revolutionary Review!* and sign autographs. Cast members smoke, drink Vodka, and never smile.

Building Exterior: A scale replica of St. Basil's Cathedral, but three of the spires are re-arranged, so there is one large one and two smaller ones off to each side, forming a "Hidden Mickey."

The Attraction: A 20-minute 360 degree movie entitled *Communism: How Great is it, Anyway?* Screens surround the standing viewer, so guests see the workers' paradise that was the Soviet Union first hand. Dipp pitched the following sequences as helicopter shots…

"Tanks rolling through Red Square. Look at 'em go!"

"Tired farmers in the fields, handing over their crops to government officials. Keep on farming, boys!"

"Empty grocery store aisles. The food is so good, they can't keep it in stock!"

"Dirty children wandering the streets alone. Probably gettin' into scrapes!"

"Siberian men freezing in a wooden shack. Vodka will keep 'em warm!"

Exit: The film lets out into The People's Nourishment Distribution Center, a restaurant featuring a wide variety of cabbage soups with "a sprinkling of shoe heel, just like Mama Olga made." Guests can also order a fruit salad (grapes and cantaloupe slices).

Feedback: "I appreciate Hidden Mickeys. That is all I have to say about the proposal at this time." –Morton

THE FUR-TURE OF PETS

Year Developed: 1977
Intended Destination: Future World, EPCOT Center
Intended Sponsor: Ralston Purina
Original Assignment: Create sponsored attraction ideas for Future World – a section of EPCOT Center celebrating advancements in science, technology, health and exploration.

Attraction Summary: Dogs are man's best... friend-o-trons? A *fur*-out ride through the *fur*-ture of *fur*-ry pets in the *fur*-off year two thousand *fur*-ve (2005)!

Dippspiration: As a kid, Walt enjoyed putting doll costumes on squirrels and rats to see if they'd sing and dance. Walt got bit and went through "rabies fer a spell," but Dipp always thought that was a fun idea. Which got Dipp thinking, "What would Walt imagine was the future for the family pet?"

Theme: In Dipp's words: "When yer livin' on Mars, how'll yer dog fetch the morning paper without a rocket in his posterior? Mark my words, in 30 years, pets will be more than companions. They'll be computer-panions! I call it pet-gineering, and this new ride fer *Fur-ture World* is gonna be one giant leap fer man's best friend!"

Building Exterior: The ride building is beige and brownish orange ("the colors of the future," Dipp explained) and shaped like a drive-in Pizza Hut ("the shape of the future," Dipp explained).

Line Queue: Guest enter the PetPort, a transportation station whose sole purpose is to take visitors on a journey through the future of pets. On the walls are paintings of important moments in future pet history, like the inauguration of the first dog senator and the first goldfish wrongly convicted of murder.

The Attraction: The optimistic dark ride shows visions of the future. In one room, a family enjoys a beautiful spring day on Mars, while their cat – with a chip in its brain – does their taxes. The next room is downtown Mars, where folks place bets on the MMA (Magnificent Mauling Animals) robo-death main event: Jumpin' Joe Gerbil vs. Knifey Rabbit. Back on earth, dogs with jet packs build a skyscraper – the largest one ever, for the greatest company ever, Ralston Purina! The ride ends with a zippy, throwback Tin Pan Alley song...

Kittens full of bolts and nuts
Dogs with rockets up their butts!
Hamsters like you've never seen-a
Glory to Ralston Purina

Bow wow, oh wow!
Look at 'em now!
It's the Fur-ture of Pets

Exit: After the ride, "every guest receives a free dog!"

Feedback: "Your spelling has improved. I only found 15 obvious errors." –Morton

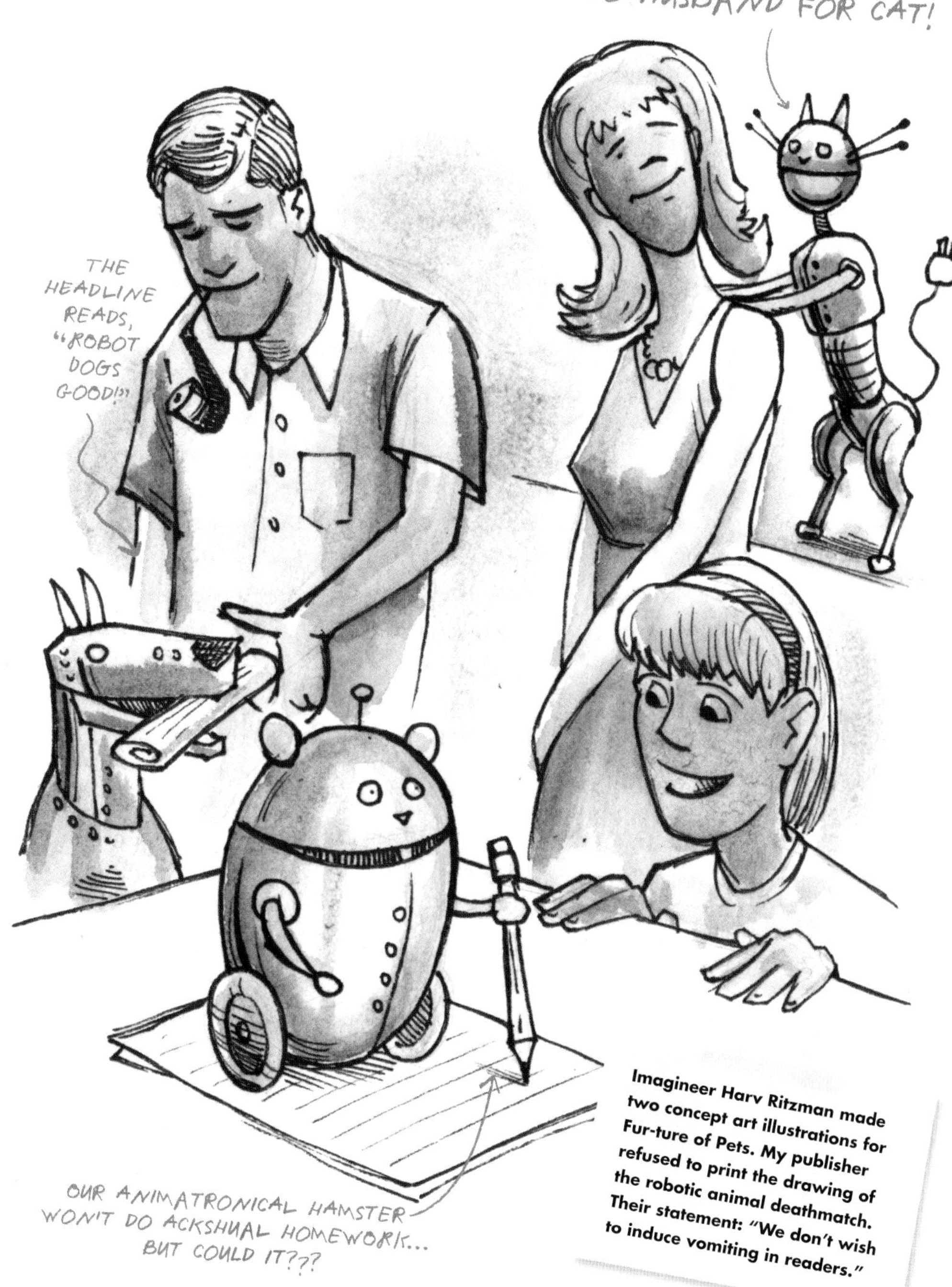

CAT MASSAGE IS SO ENJOYABLE, SHE WILL LEAVE HUSBAND FOR CAT!
THE HEADLINE READS, "ROBOT DOGS GOOD!"
OUR ANIMATRONICAL HAMSTER WON'T DO ACKSHUAL HOMEWORK... BUT COULD IT???

Imagineer Harv Ritzman made two concept art illustrations for Fur-ture of Pets. My publisher refused to print the drawing of the robotic animal deathmatch. Their statement: "We don't wish to induce vomiting in readers."

Dipp and illustrator Harv Ritzman had a disagreement over how to portray the wrapped baby. Dipp wanted to show him breathing comfortably, whereas Harv wanted the baby to be taking its final breaths. So, they compromised.

DOESN'T KNOW WHAT'S HAPPENING

ONE BABY, SEALED AND DELIVERED TO A TUBE!

BUBBLE WRAP BABY STATION

BUBBLE WRAP IS THE NANNY OF PLASTICS

IDEA #1507

BUBBLE WRAP BABY STATION

Year Developed: 1977
Intended Destination: Future World, EPCOT Center
Intended Sponsor: Sealed Air, makers of Bubble Wrap
Original Assignment: A special assignment from Morton: "Try and design something that would be useful for guests. Think practical. Like a new type of water fountain, or a way to obtain money from guests faster."

Attraction Summary: We've got child care at EPCOT all "wrapped up." The future of babysitting is bubble-sitting!

Dippspiration: Dipp liked to walk around Disneyland and observe the guests in action, as Walt often advised. One day, Dipp made a startling revelation watching adults walk around the park with their children: "Every parent hates their babies! No one wants to lug 'em around a hot theme park all day. They're dead weight, and ya can't go on the best rides with one. What EPCOT needs is fun, safe, and futuristic child care. A new way to dump yer younglins."

Building Exterior: Spherical and clear with giant bubbles you could push inward. Like the whole building was enveloped in bubble wrap. "It gives y'all the aura of safetude (sic)," as Dipp put it.

The Attraction: At the counter, parents hand over their baby to "The Specialist." In Phase 1, The Specialist gently and efficiently wraps the baby in several layers of bubble wrap, being careful not to wrap the front of the face.

In Phase 2, The Specialist places the wrapped baby into a large clear bubble wrap envelope with air holes.

In Phase 3, The Specialist stores the twice wrapped baby in a plexiglass pod with air holes, the door of which is locked with a key. "Just be sure to remember yer pod key when y'all return to de-wrap yer baby," Dipp cautioned.

Feedback: "Thanks for the free bubble wrap, Dipp. Have you talked with the Sealed Air people to see whether they recommend wrapping a human child in several layers of their product?" –Morton

"Every parent hates their babies!"

THE UNIVERSE OF ENERGY: COPIED BY XEROX

Year Developed: 1980
Intended Destination: Future World, EPCOT Center
Intended Sponsor: Xerox
Original Assignment: Create sponsored attraction ideas for Future World – a section of EPCOT Center celebrating advancements in science, technology, health and exploration.

Attraction Summary: It's an exact copy of The Universe of Energy, brought to you by Xerox, the copy experts.

Dippspiration: There were plans in place for a ride called "the Universe of Energy," about the past and future of various energy sources, sponsored by Exxon. This ride was green-lit for EPCOT, which Dipp knew because he found photocopied schematics in the collection tray of the office Xerox machine. That's when a lightbulb went off! Literally, a bulb went off in the copy room. Dipp also had an idea...

Building Exterior: An exact replica of the Universe of Energy pavilion, built directly across from the original Universe of Energy. Same mirror walls, reflecting pool, everything you love.

Pre-Show: It's the lobby with those cube screens. Again, exactly like the Universe of Energy.

The Attraction: In Dipp's words: "So here's what we do. We're buildin' the Universe of Energy – a great attraction, by the by. My favorite part is the 12 minute video where y'all see scientists lookin' for oil in various places. Kids'll get a hoot outta that! So what we do is, we build an exact replica of the Universe of Energy right next door to the Universe of Energy! Sponsored by Xerox, cause in the future, they'll be able to copy anythin'. Clothin', food, even folks like y'all and me! So we build a brick fer brick, solar panel fer solar panel copy. We even install video monitors so the cast members in the replica can imitate the exact movements and expressions of the cast members in the original.

Heck, I bet we can get Exxon to co-sponsor the copy along with Xerox. Two sponsors fer one ride, and we don't even have to design anythin' new! Same theater carts, same pro-oil script – I love oil, don't everybody? – same animatronic dinosaurs, same excitin' shots of windmill farms. Maybe we make a few tweaks to the song...

Feel the flow (again)
Here we go (again)
Through the Universe of Energy
(The Replica)
Feel it grow (again)
See it glow (once more)
It's the Universe of Xeroxin'."

Feedback: "It's unoriginal, but I guess that was the point. So... good job?" –Morton

In the original version of the concept art below, Harv Ritzman had the guest scratching his head so hard, he scratched through his skin, skull, and was poking his brain matter. Dipp thought it was "fun," but worried the spraying blood might distract from the core concept.

Imagineer Harv Ritzman drunkenly crashed a tractor into the Glendale office as reference for the above illustration. (An odd excuse, as he had already completed the drawing when he did it.) Harv was forcibly retired and sent to Chip 'n' Dale's Home for the Criminally Insane in WDW. Dipp was sad to see Harv go, until Harv threatened to disembowel Dipp with a butter knife in the cafeteria.

MOONSHINE MOUNTAIN

Year Developed: 1983
Intended Destination: Critter Country, Disneyland
Original Assignment: Design an E-Ticket attraction for Critter Country.

Attraction Summary: In this rowdy flume ride, where the water is "ackshual (sic) moonshine," the Country Bears confront Ted about his infamous drinkin' problem!

Dippspiration: Dipp describes this proposal as "semi-automagraphicalary (sic)."

Story: During the pitch, a hammered Dipp said this ride would finally solve the great mystery of the Country Bears: "Where does Ted... the bear... get moonshine to fill his... jugs?"

Building Exterior: A tree covered mountain in a Missouri summer with a magical, sparkling river of moonshine running through it.

The Attraction: Guests board a log flume and head on down the moonshine river. Remembering an old idea he had for Stinky Drinky Pirates, which he remembered Walt liking very much, the water in the ride would be actual, drinkable moonshine. Guests could buy souvenir corn jugs and "get bashed while they splash."

After a few heart racing drops, guests enter rooms of animatronic critters, who set-up the story. The Country Bears confront their bandmate Ted about his drinking problem. So Ted decides to drive up Moonshine Mountain in his tractor, "intent on fillin' up his jug." The Bears chase after him, because they knew he was "headed fer a craaaaaaaash!"

As the flume rises higher, the bears sing classic country songs to coax him down. Songs like: "Drunk as a Skunk (Pee-Yew!)," "Just an Ol' Fashioned Country Addiction," and "It's a Physical Disease (Oh My, Oh Me's)." Ted doesn't listen to the advice of his friends, and drives his tractor over a steep waterfall... and guests follow him down!

Luckily, they all land safely in a lazy river! "See? Ted don't have to change nothin' about his self," Dipp screamed to a horrified room of Imagineers.

Exit: Guests are let off into the Country Bear's Secret Shack, an interactive moonshine distillery where kids make and bottle moonshine for their parents.

Feedback: After Dipp passed out on the floor and pissed his pants during the presentation, Morton asked, "Is he dead?"

(1984-
1992)

DIPP DISNEY & MICHAEL EISNER: BEST FRIENDS

In 1984, Michael Eisner became the new CEO of The Walt Disney Company. After a successful run as a top creative executive at Paramount, Eisner was brought in to revitalize the House of Mouse. He was charming, funny, highly impulsive – and about to make a new friend in the Imagineering department.

The weekend after the Moonshine Mountain debacle, Dipp cleaned up his act. He went cold turkey, literally pouring all his moonshine out into his backyard to be lapped up by his pet turkeys, which were very cold due to the malfunctioning AC unit Dipp installed in their pen. He attempted to go to his first AA meeting (intentionally), but ended up at AAA Auto Body in Burbank. Luckily, one of the mechanics there was a recovering alcoholic and agreed to be Dipp's sponsor.

Both Dipp and Morgan were excited to come to work that Monday. Dipp regained his signature skip and whistle, and Morgan was ready to fire him for good. However, this also happened to be the day Michael Eisner first toured the Glendale office. The first person Michael met was Dipp, who came to work rolling in a giant tire as a pitch for a new EPCOT ride called Tiremobiles: The Future of Cars are Tires (Presented by Goodyear). Eisner was delighted, called Dipp "an old fashioned showman" and "a valuable lifeline to Walt Disney, the man." Eisner instantly promoted Dipp from Creative Consultant to Vice President of Creative Consulting and bought Dipp a titanium vault for his iron contract. Morton was devastated.

Dipp and Eisner became fast friends, and Dipp encouraged Eisner to become the creative beacon at Imagineering. "I think poor ol' Mort-o could use a little R&R in Neverland," Dipp smiled and winked. Eisner winked back, then later that day fired Morton in front of his family. When Dipp explained he just thought Morton could use a vacation, Eisner re-hired Morton as Junior Vice President of

Dipp and Eisner attend the annual Malfunctioning Animatron Bonfire Jamboree.

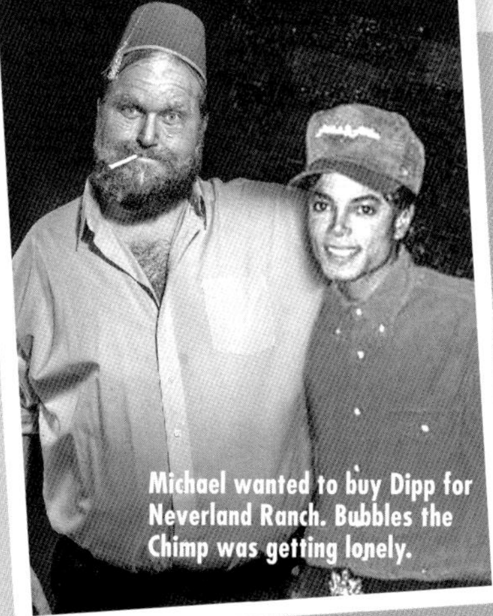
Michael wanted to buy Dipp for Neverland Ranch. Bubbles the Chimp was getting lonely.

Creative Consulting, so he would once again report directly to Dipp. The Mayor of Disneyland was impeached.

First order of business: Disney was set to build a theme park in Europe, bolstered by the success of Tokyo Disneyland. Michael Eisner was presented with a list of 1,200 possible European locations for the park. When Eisner asked Dipp for his advice, Dipp didn't even look at the sheet. "Build it in Paris," said Dipp. "They're so darn stuffy over there. A little Disney magic would do 'em good, and will do good profits, too." Eisner didn't need any more convincing.

One of Michael Eisner's first moves as CEO was to bring outside pop culture into the Disney parks. "Pinnochio is great, I love that guy," Eisner once remarked at a shareholders meeting. "But is he hot with teens? My nose would be growing if I said 'yes.' So I'll say the opposite: 'No.'" He placed Dipp on teams that worked with Michael Jackson, George Lucas, Jim Henson and other people Eisner liked to name drop at cocaine-fueled Hollywood parties.

However, despite Eisner's trust and love of Dipp, his ideas still weren't being seriously developed or making it to the parks. One day, Dipp expressed his frustrations to Eisner in a private meeting.

"I know I have an iron contract," Dipp confessed. "But honestly, I'm not sure why my office didn't get moved to the secondary supply room in the sub-basement prison years ago. I would've been outta all y'all's hairs."

"I know why I value you, Dipp," Eisner responded. "It's because you inspire me. You're such a colossal failure, and I mean that in the best possible way. You say the worst idea in the room with incredible consistency. The result is that other Imagineers open up and just throw ideas out, because they know what they say can't possibly be worse than what you pitched. Failure is the key to the creative process, and you're the master of failure. It takes a special kind of bravery to be willing to make a fool of yourself every day for, what, 30 years? I envy your tenacity. Of course, every idea I come up with is solid gold, failure-proof. Here's one right now... The Go Network. I don't know what it is yet, but I do know it's gonna be incredible."

Dipp realized his whole life was spent in pursuit of greatness. He tried to live up to his position and the Disney name. Unfortunately after 30 years, even his best ideas were like the aftermath of a Main Street Parade: horseshit.

And then, Dipp lost his train of thought, so he challenged himself to a whistling contest.

If we can dream it, we can do it.

Dipp takes top honors in a whistling contest against himself.

IDEA #3905

The Jackson 5-Dimensions

Year Developed: 1984
Intended Destination: Future World, EPCOT Center
Original Assignment: Design an attraction based around pop superstar Michael Jackson.

Attraction Summary: In this "5D" movie, Jackie, Tito, Jermaine, Marlon, and don't forget lil' Michael, all go on an outer-space adventure riding a magic rainbow.

Dippspiration: Dipp wanted to impress Eisner and get off on the right foot. So he began researching Jackson, listening to his albums chronologically: *ABC*, *Maybe Tomorrow*, *Lookin' Through Windows*... He didn't make it to *Off the Wall* before the kickoff meeting with Jackson, but Dipp was already inspired by what he heard.

Pre-Show: While guests wait for the next screening, there's a pre-show video promoting The Jackson 5's hot new album *Victory*, proclaiming there would be many, many more albums to come from the pop supergroup.

The Attraction: The film opens with Goo Jackson, the Jackson 5's evil alien warlord father, who zaps our heroes with laser rays until they vomit magic space rainbows on stage for their adoring fans. Goo's tentacles often pop out of the screen to reassuringly stroke the heads and faces of audience members.

Tito, the hero of the story, has the idea to make rainbow surfboards for themselves, and use them to get away from Goo. Thus begins "a real musical space race" between the evil Goo Jackson and his children, where they must dodge meteors (along with the audience!) and blast "star demons" while singing slightly modified versions of their hits, like "ABC (Alpha Base Command)," "I Want You Back (to My Rainbow Prison)" and "I'll Be There (in Galactic Quadrant 97Z)."

At the heart of the story is a message: No matter what, through thick and thin, the Jacksons always stick together – no Jackson left behind! Their motto? "We're equally talented brothers who will never break up!"

Feedback: After his presentation, Jackson reportedly offered to buy Dipp from Disney for $2 million as a new best friend for Bubbles. Michael thought Dipp was "funny."

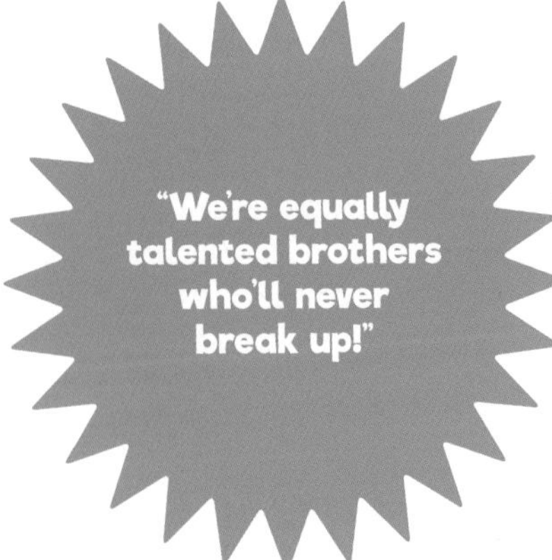
"We're equally talented brothers who'll never break up!"

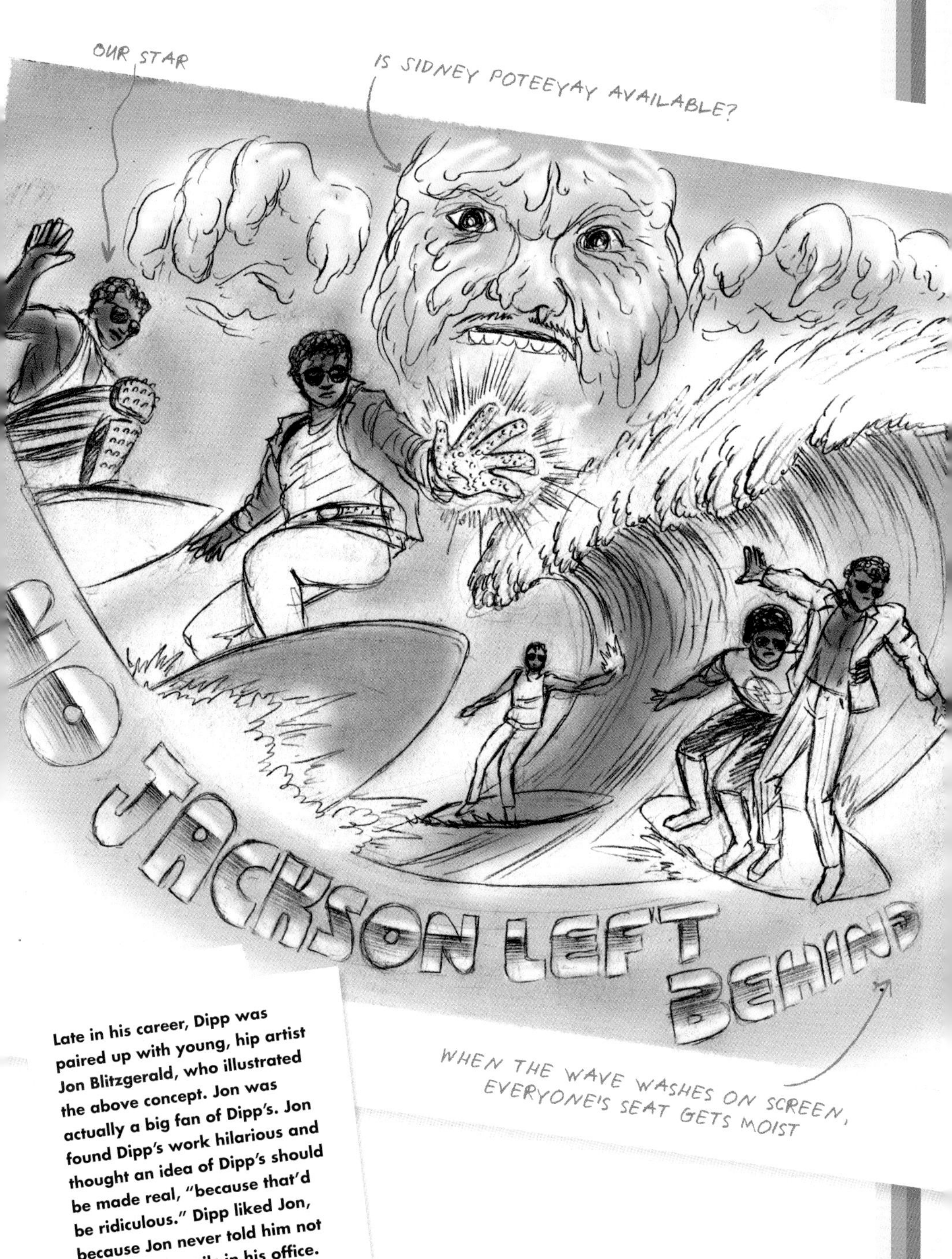

Late in his career, Dipp was paired up with young, hip artist Jon Blitzgerald, who illustrated the above concept. Jon was actually a big fan of Dipp's. Jon found Dipp's work hilarious and thought an idea of Dipp's should be made real, "because that'd be ridiculous." Dipp liked Jon, because Jon never told him not to clip his toenails in his office.

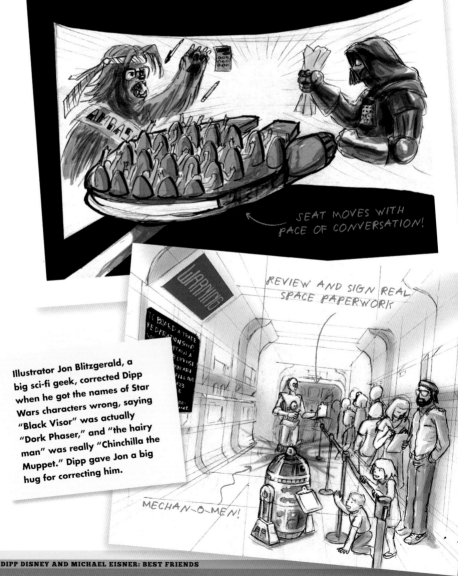

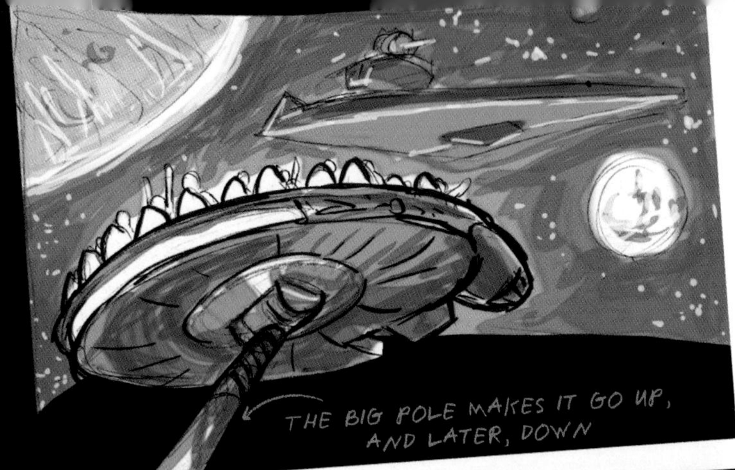

Illustrator Jon Blitzgerald, a big sci-fi geek, corrected Dipp when he got the names of Star Wars characters wrong, saying "Black Visor" was actually "Dork Phaser," and "the hairy man" was really "Chinchilla the Muppet." Dipp gave Jon a big hug for correcting him.

IDEA #4322

Star Wars: Blast-Off to Bureaucracy!

Year Developed: 1985
Intended Destination: Tomorrowland, Disneyland
Original Assignment: Work with the team at Industrial Lights and Magic to develop a motion ride based on *Star Wars*.

Attraction Summary: **In a galaxy far, far away, ride along with interplanetary economic negotiators in this high speed motion simulator ride!**

Dippspiration: At the Disney cafeteria, Dipp overheard someone say that science fiction is often just a fantastic version of today's reality. So he researched and found an article in a newspaper he thought was especially boring and made it… "fantastical!"

A bit of research Dipp neglected to do: see any of the *Star Wars* films. Dipp pieced the narrative together through toy commercials and a holiday special he watched half asleep.

Building Exterior: A gray space station, tall and rectangular, like an IRS building.

Line Queue: A series of gray "futuristical" (sic) hallways. "In the walkway, guests run into the gold robot and his friend, whose name is numbers. They tell ya that the blonde one and the hairy man are in trouble, cause Black Visor broke a space protectorship agreement, and now everyone is real angered."

The Attraction: Guests enter the motion simulator and rocket from planet to planet "doin' alien things, like negotiatin' treaties, settin' up blockades, and enforcin' the protectorship agreement Black Visor hates so much!" However, when you're discovered by Darth Vader – "who hates tariffs, treaties and what have ya!" – you have to bring Vader back to the negotiation table using "all the different Forces, including Bea Arthur."

Feedback: Although the team at ILM were immediately dismissive of Blast-Off to Bureaucracy, George Lucas loved it. He just knew there was something magical and important about the idea of an Intergalactic Trade Federation.

Lucas thanked Dipp profusely for the idea, and asked if he could tinker with it a little. Dipp told Lucas he could have it. "Whatever you turn that idea into, I'm sure *Star Wars* fans will love it," Dipp smiled.

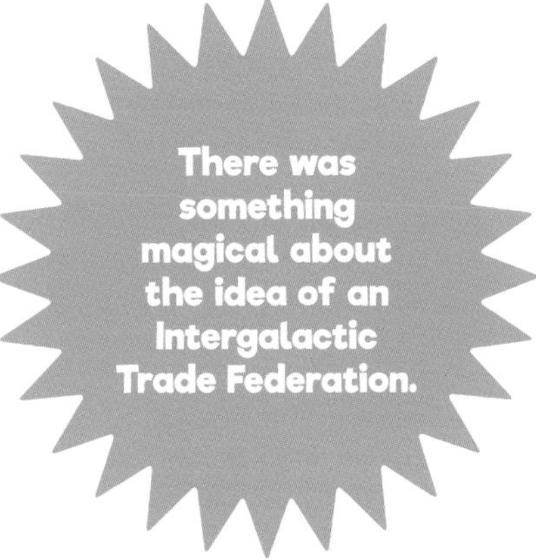
There was something magical about the idea of an Intergalactic Trade Federation.

The Magic of Disney Live-Action

Year Developed: 1985
Intended Destination: Disney's MGM Studios
Original Assignment: Develop ideas for a new movie theme park with attractions based on golden age and behind-the-scenes Hollywood.

Attraction Summary: **A prop museum and walking tour about how Disney makes its beloved live-action films.**

Dippspiration: Dipp loved the movies. His favorites were classics like *Plan 9 From Outer Space*, *Santa Claus Conquers the Martians*, and Disney's *The Parent Switch*, where two identical twin sisters switch bodies with their identical twin parents.

Building Exterior: A real life Hollywood soundstage: beige, rectangular, and with one potted plant outside. ("Who knows how many 'celebs' ashed their cigarettes in that plant?")

Pre-Show: Guests watch an introductory film starring secret agent Condorman, tasked by the CIA to locate That Darn Cat, who unwittingly swallowed a top secret microchip. When That Darn Cat enters the Disney lot, Condorman inadvertently takes a studio tour, and learns how Disney live action classics are made.

The Attraction: A walking tour mixed with videos guides guests through four different rooms of a studio, each containing cast members "play actin' as Hollywood big shot types."

The first room is The Executive's Office, where a slick producer pitches a powerful executive his bold new idea: "Eight more Herbie the Love Bug movies!" The executive hands him a bag with a dollar sign on it and they shake hands.

In The Producer's Mansion, the producer snorts magic powder poolside, which helps him finish pre-production.

On The Set, Condorman watches a pivotal scene, where Herbie meets his zany twin "bugger" (bug brother) voiced by Dom DeLuise! The director is fast asleep on set, dreaming up more great ideas.

Finally, in The Edit Room, shots get spliced together and put into a film cannister. This is also where Condorman catches That Darn Cat, but decides to let him go, "so there can be sequels!"

After the tour, there's a gallery of props from cherished Disney live action films. On display are "the flubber from *Son of Flubber*, the black hole from *The Black Hole*, and costumes from our new horror film, *Return to Oz*."

Exit: Guests exit the gallery into the Mandatory Union Break food stand, where they can "get a 'grip'... on a sandwich!" Enjoy their signature Fruit Salad (grapes and cantaloupe slices).

Feedback: Dipp pitched the idea to Eisner during a "Hollywood power lunch" at a historic Sizzler in Culver City. When Dipp asked Eisner what he thought, he said his surf & turf was "rubbery." Then Eisner complimented Dipp on his idea for "what was it? Some kind of tour? Fantastic."

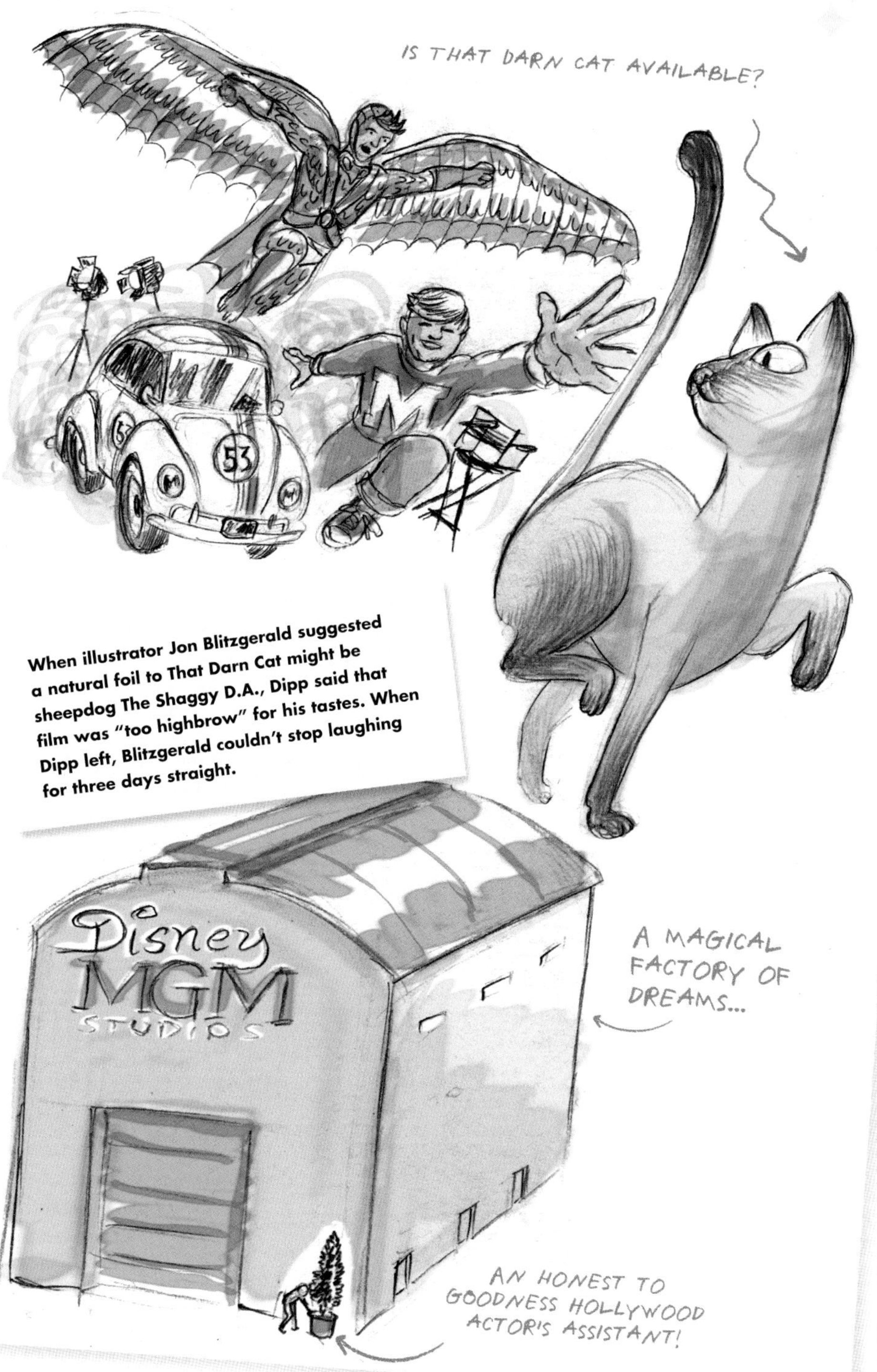

IS THAT DARN CAT AVAILABLE?
53
Disney
MGM
STUDIOS
A MAGICAL FACTORY OF DREAMS...
AN HONEST TO GOODNESS HOLLYWOOD ACTOR'S ASSISTANT!

When illustrator Jon Blitzgerald suggested a natural foil to That Darn Cat might be sheepdog The Shaggy D.A., Dipp said that film was "too highbrow" for his tastes. When Dipp left, Blitzgerald couldn't stop laughing for three days straight.

HE PLAYS ALL THE HITS, LIKE THE MONSTER MASH, AND OTHER "GROOVY" MASHES

STAY OFF LAWN

THEY WON'T!

To help inspire Imagineer Jon Blitzgerald to illustrate the above concept art, Dipp silently stroked a shotgun in character while Jon worked at his drawing board. For the first time in his life, Jon experienced true terror. "Why so serious today, Jon Boy?" Dipp asked.

Get Off My Lawn!

Year Developed: 1987
Intended Destination: Pleasure Island
Original Assignment: Develop nightclub ideas for Pleasure Island, an entertainment district aimed at adults.

Attraction Summary: **At this outdoor club, dance the night away on a grumpy old man's lawn, as he scowls and polishes his shotgun.**

Dippspiration: Dipp was an old man, but having a patron in Eisner made him feel young, like he was in his mid-60s again. Over the years, many executives at Disney respectfully encouraged him to retire and get off Disney property, but he never listened. He felt young, no matter what his back, face, or liver were trying to tell him.

Theme: In Dipp's words: "It's a simple fact of nature. Young people love loafin' around on elderly men's lawns. I don't know why, but I say, if we're talking about a place where young folks can really cut loose, let's give 'em what they want. Lawns!"

The Attraction: Get Off My Lawn! is an outdoor dance party. The setting is the overgrown suburban lawn of Mr. Bruthers, "a grumpy ol' coot if there ever was one!" He's in his 80s, rocking on the porch polishing his beloved shotgun named Bessy May Valentine III. On the lawn, there's a boombox blasting hot dance music, like "the disco, the fruug, that sorta thing" and everyone is dancing on Mr. Bruthers' lawn.

He stares daggers at the dancers, polishing that gun. A couple times a night, he fires his gun into the air and everyone scatters. "But it's just fer show. Ten minutes later and the kids are back, break-scamperin' harder than ever before."

Since it was a lawn-themed club, Dipp suggested a mystery hose. The bartender presents the guest with the hose and turns it on for a minute, and it's all you can drink! What type of alcohol will come out? "Could be mint julep, Miller Light, white wine... but I hope it's moonshine!" At which point in his presentation, Dipp took out a jug with a hose funnel attached and drank a few glasses worth of "virgin moonshine" (cough syrup mixed with soy sauce).

True Story: Dipp began his presentation by taking a shotgun out of a duffel bag and swung it around for show. After a half an hour of panic and hiding behind chairs, Dipp finally convinced his fellow Imagineers that he wasn't going to shoot them. It was "just a lil' ol' prop." A fully-loaded prop with the prop safety off, but a prop nonetheless.

Later, Eisner heard that Dipp really "shook things up" at the Pleasure Island meeting. "Good!" Eisner said. "That's what we're paying him for."

Judge Doom's Toon Execution Room

Year Developed: 1988
Intended Destination: Mickey's ToonTown, Disneyland
Original Assignment: Develop a theme park attraction centered around the smash hit film *Who Framed Roger Rabbit?*

Attraction Summary: **In this live multimedia show, witness sinister Judge Doom play judge, jury and ultimately executioner to a series of unfortunate cartoon characters.**

Dippspiration: Dipp loved the movies, but was now sleeping through more and more of them. He only managed to stay awake through one scene of *Who Framed Roger Rabbit?*, and was surprised by how dark it was for a Disney feature. Still, if the public wanted a terrifying experience at Disneyland, who was Dipp to deny them?

Theme: This idea was based on the sequence where Judge Doom grabs an innocent, squeaky cartoon shoe and drops him into "the dip," murdering him. In this attraction, guests watch Doom murder toon after toon in person, "fulfillin' the modern theme park family's desire to see the movies come to life!"

Building Exterior: An intimidating gray stone fortress dubbed ToonTown Jerk Jail.

Line Queue: Guests walk through the prison, passing the cells of dangerous criminal toons awaiting execution, like The Wicked Queen (Attempted Murder), Mr. Toad (Vehicular Manslaughter), Robin Hood and his Merry Men (Domestic Terrorism).

The Attraction: Baloo the Prison Warden (a costumed character) escorts guests to their seats in the Execution Room's viewing chamber. A cast member comes out playing Judge Doom, and using projections on the glass, it looks like he's actually interacting with cartoon characters, dropping them into the dip.

Judge Doom pretends to hold a frightened, struggling mop from *Fantasia* and says, "For the crime of making the floor wet before I started walking, causing me to trip in a comical manner, I hereby sentence you to... the dip." Then the cast member mimes shoving the mop into an empty vat, while the screen projects the mop shaking violently in terror.

Dipp explains that Doom only executes toons who caused him mild discomfort that day. "That's what makes him a bad man in my book. He'd kill Jiminy Cricket fer whistlin' too loud or Thumper fer lookin' at him funny. And with this attraction, he'll get his chance!"

Feedback: Eisner said he liked parts of this idea, to the shock and amazement of the other Imagineers. (Even Dipp wasn't sure about this one, though he enjoyed saying the word "dip" so many times.)

Specifically, Eisner liked the idea of "a scary show that'll terrify children. Maybe some kind of alien encounter? Whatever it is, make it violent!"

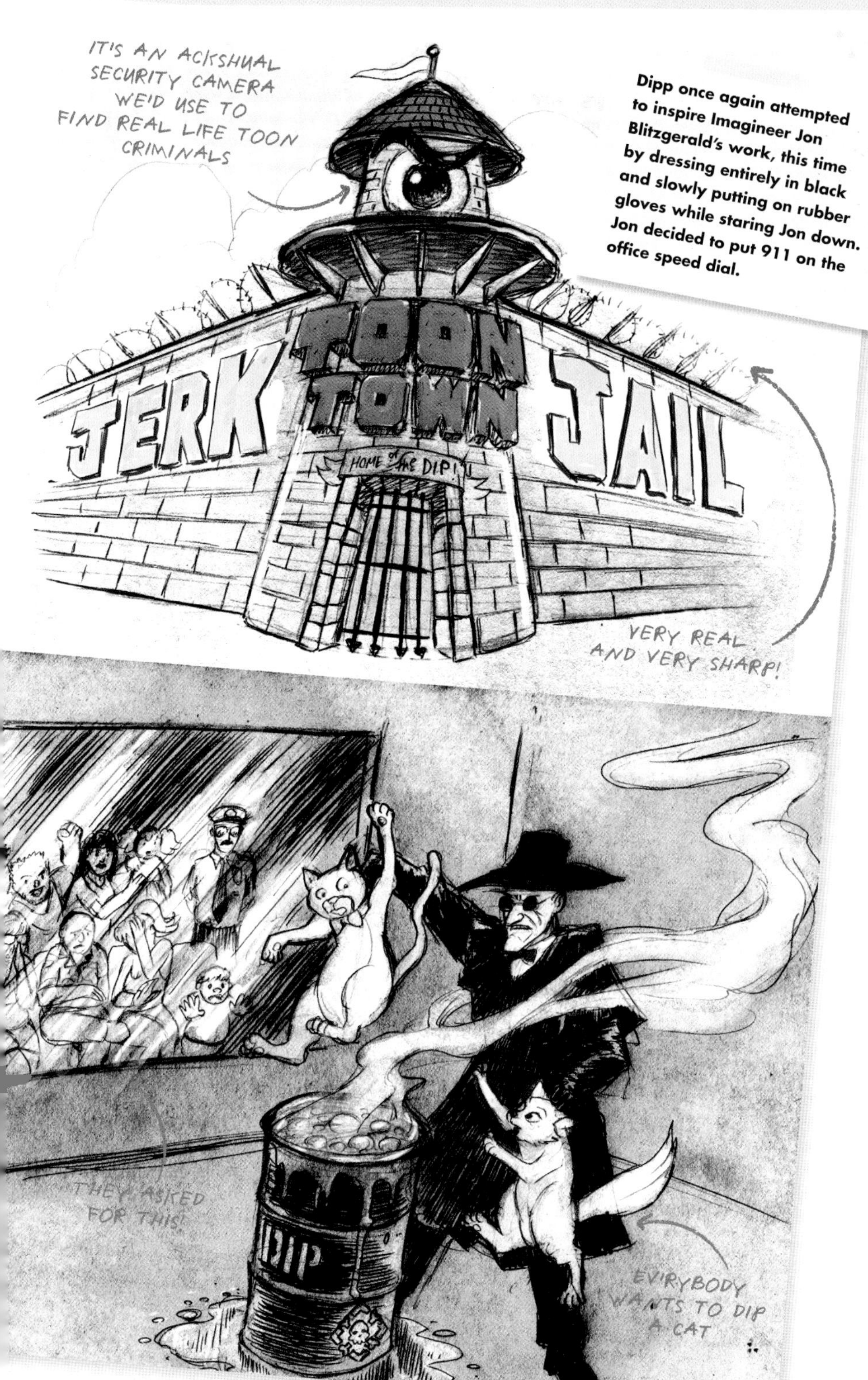
IT'S AN ACKSHUAL SECURITY CAMERA WE'D USE TO FIND REAL LIFE TOON CRIMINALS
JERK TOON TOWN JAIL
HOME of the DIP!
VERY REAL AND VERY SHARP!
THEY ASKED FOR THIS!
DIP
EVERYBODY WANTS TO DIP A CAT

Dipp once again attempted to inspire Imagineer Jon Blitzgerald's work, this time by dressing entirely in black and slowly putting on rubber gloves while staring Jon down. Jon decided to put 911 on the office speed dial.

PIG CRIES FOR MONEY
CURTAINS, LIKE IN LEGIMINATE THEATERS
MUPPETS take CENTRAL FLORIDA
ACTORS IN COSTUMES, PLAY ACTING LIKE THEY WAS MUPPETS

Imagineer Jon Blitzgerald FedExed this piece into Imagineering, along with his resignation. "I sincerely apologize to Dipp for laughing at him and his work," Jon said. "Now tell him to stay the hell away from me!" Dipp told a colleague he was surprised by the sudden resignation, but thought Jon was "a real great kid."

The Muppets Take Central Florida

Year Developed: 1989
Intended Destination: Disney's MGM Studios
Original Assignment: Develop an attraction starring The Muppets for Disney's MGM Studios.

Attraction Summary: Join Jim Henson's Muppets for a hilarious live musical about the gang settling into the slow pace of regular life in Orlando, FL.

Dippspiration: Though his fellow Imagineers were nervous about meeting with Jim Henson, Dipp claimed he understood the Muppet formula. "All the Muppet movies are about them goin' somewhere. On the road, or Jew York City, or that fancy town in Europe. Where they speak funny. Brittsylvania? Yup, that's the one."

The Attraction: It's a live musical show about The Muppets making a permanent home in Orlando to work at Disney World. The Muppets are portrayed as costumed characters, moving along to a sync track. "If y'all record it, y'all and yer Muppetorman (sic) puppet masters don't have to do every performance yerselves," Dipp explained to Jim Henson.

In Dipp's words: "Ribbit the Frog is touring retirement communities. He's the smart, sensible one. He doesn't wanna end up in some horrible swamp when he 'croaks.' I see Ribbit as the leader of yer little group.

Miss Pig got her own TV show in Florida. She's on the public channel as a televangelist. She's real good at doin' the cryin' where the mascara runs. That's big now in that world.

Meanwhile, there's a story with Fonzie the Boar and Blue Nose where they spend all day lost in the aisle of a K-Mart. That happened to me recently. It can happen to anyone, really. They make those stores so gosh darn big! And that's good for Fonzie, because he can make wiseacres about it. Like, 'We're so lost, my compass points to Good Luck!' Somethin' fun like that.

The Electric Band plays at the Hometown Buffet, which would be a good gig for them. They get paid in food, I think. Ralph the Moleman gets stuck in traffic. He'd probably sing a song called 'Holy Moleman'… holy moleman… holy moleman..."

True Story: When Henson started coughing during the meeting, Dipp said it sounded pretty bad, and suggested going to a doctor. Henson, who later asked Eisner if Dipp was "diagnosed psychotic or just regular crazy," declined to take Dipp's advice.

Surprise Elephant Poo!

Year Developed: 1990
Intended Destination: Animal Kingdom
Original Assignment: Develop ideas for "Wild Kingdom," an animal and conservation themed park project inspired by Walt's nature documentaries.

Attraction Summary: **Watch your step! To make the safari theme more authentic, cast members place piles of real elephant dung in walkways throughout the park.**

Proposed Slogan: "If y'all get some on yer shoe, just remember... it's a 'smelly' world after all."

True Story: Dipp brought a box of elephant shit into the meeting and dumped it all over the table. He warmly smiled at everyone in the room, then left without making his actual proposal.

It's a 'smelly' world after all.

Dipp was trying to find his new pet snake, which slithered into the desk of long-sense retired Imagineer Nick Javits – and Dipp discovered this drawing. So he decided to pitch it to Michael Eisner. At Disney, no idea ever goes to waste.

DOES THIS REALLY NEED ANY EXPLANATION? WELL, IN CASE IT DOES, IT'S ELEPHANT DUNG

(1993 - ????)

LEGACY OF A DIPP

The magic lives on!

In 1993, Dipp celebrated his 30th year at Imagineering and his 90th birthday. He was given a cake with Cinderella's castle drawn on in frosting by his co-workers. This sparked an idea for Dipp. What if you turned Cinderella's Castle into a birthday cake? The idea was met with polite laughter and mild applause. His young colleagues were impressed that he could still have new ideas, despite being so old.

Later that year, a co-worker made the mistake of asking Dipp if he could get him a coffee from the break room. Dipp got lost and never resurfaced. Some say he died drinking turpentine, thinking it was moonshine. Others say he went on to design Twister… Ride it Out for Universal Studios. I like to think he finally found that pack of family cigarettes and brought them home to Bubbles, his children, and his children's children. But I'd put my money on the turpentine thing.

No one knows what happened to Morton Boggs either, because everyone kinda forgot about him.

In 1994, the Imagineers were coming up with big ideas to celebrate Disneyland's 25th anniversary, and after a long debate, they settled on Dipp's idea to turn Cinderella's Castle into a giant birthday cake. It was the only attraction idea of Dipp's that made it into the parks. AllEars.net described the castle's cake makeover as "thankfully temporary" and Yesterland.com called it "objectionable."

Dipp's "best" idea.

* * *

When a few of Dipp's ideas leaked onto the blog Disney: The Promised Land in 2009, it created a surge of interest in Dipp's life. There are a small number of Disney fans who call themselves "*Dipp*ciples," and claim that Dipp's ideas

Can you find all the Hidden Dippies? There are hundreds in the Disney parks.

were genius and ahead of their time. A group of ten Dippciples even attempted to stage one of Dipp's most controversial ideas on Main Street – a protest parade celebrating civil rights using costumed character versions of Martin Luther King Jr. and Malcolm X called World of Coloreds. These zealous, white fans were quickly escorted from the premises.

Disney decided to publically acknowledge Dipp's legacy the following year, when they created a collectable pin for the Vietnamese Jungle Cruise, depicting Dipp and Baloo in camo gear burning down a village. The pin was taken out of Disneyland kiosks the same day it debuted, after receiving hundreds of complaints, and the company is still apologizing for that pin to this day.

There's one thing Michael Eisner or any of Dipp's superiors failed to notice about Dipp's contributions. Though Dipp's ideas were always shot down, and perhaps rightfully so, many kernels of his ideas found their way into the parks. He coined the phrase "It's a Small World," though he used it to describe a human child petting zoo. The melody of his song for "Stinky Drinky Pirates" morphed into "Yo Ho (A Pirate's Life for Me)." And though I've never heard him credited, the practice of cast members wrapping guests' babies in polyfoam for their protection can be traced back to Dipp's "notions" for EPCOT. Dipp's failures led to spectacular successes for Disney, which delight families to this day.

Besides turning Cinderella's Castle into a birthday cake, Dipp made one more direct contribution to Disney parks. Throughout Disneyland, there are a number of "Hidden Dippies," tiny cubbies where Dipp stored his illegal Missouri moonshine for years.

Disney claims they closed up all the Hidden Dippies, and disposed of the moonshine in accordance with EPA regulations, but new ones are being found all the time. Last year, a couple from Germany found one while riding the Matterhorn. They got stuck on the ride and decided to throw turkey leg bones at the Abominable Snowman's face. Suddenly, the monster vibrated, and a jug of moonshine fell out of a secret compartment in his crotch. Good ol' Dipp.

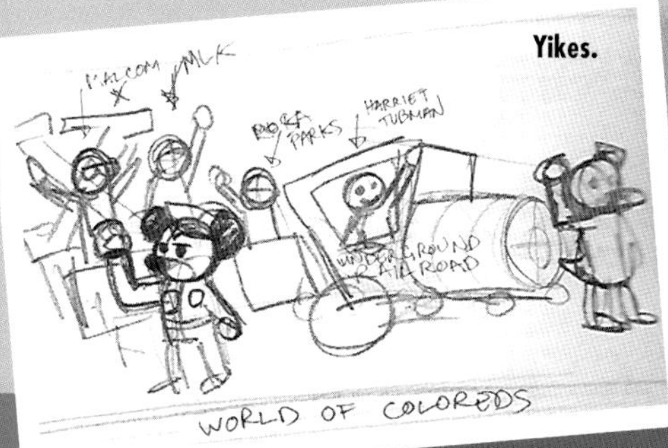

Yikes.

Acknowledgements

This book wouldn't be possible without the guidance, ideas, and patience of my wife and editor Amanda Meadows. I must've wished upon a particularly lucky star to have such a perfect partner in crime.

Thanks to my family, who inspired this book in so many ways.

Thanks to the brilliant artists – Shing Yin Khor, Elan' Trinidad, Reid Psaltis and Marc Palm, plus Mike Reddy, Spencer Dina, Aaron Alpert and Karina Caro – who labored tirelessly to bring these incredibly dumb jokes to life. And to The Devastator Author Corps who helped shape the book in significant ways: Lesley Tsina, Lee Keeler, Joan Ford, Joe Starr, Robin Higgins, Micki Grover, Meredith Donahue, Patrick Baker, Paige Weldon, Ryan Sandoval, and especially Asterios Kokkinos, the hardest working man in the goof business.

Thank you to Jeff Heimbuch, and Alex & Renita Swaekauski for bein' cool!

And a special thank you to all the brilliant Imagineers at Disney – the designers, writers, artists, builders, engineers, project managers, programmers and more – who inspired me to work hard, follow my dreams, and write this bizarre book o' gags.

Research

If you're wondering whether I did any research whatsoever, your skepticism isn't unfounded. I enjoyed reading *Designing Disney* by John Hench, *One Little Spark* and *Dream It! Do It!* (Sorry!) by Marty Sklar. I did a lot of online research on amazing sites like Designing Disney (designingdisney.com), Imagineering Disney (imagineeringdisney.com) and Theme Park Insider (themeparkinsider.com).

About the Authors

Geoffrey Golden is the bestselling author of *Frankenstein's Girlfriend*, *Snarkicide*, and co-author of *Grosslumps*. He also writes *Sesame Street* comics and (not a joke) *Disney Princess* comics. Geoffrey lives in West Hollywood, CA with his wife Amanda and their cat Gilda. His favorite Disney attractions are Alien Encounter (closed), Journey Into Imagination (the old version), and Muppet*Vision 3D (doomed).

Shing Yin Khor is a Los Angeles based cartoonist, sculptor, and swamp witch. sawdustbear.com

Elan' Trinidad and his 2009 Eisner Nomination for Best Webcomic fails to impress drunk girls at bars. Currently, Elan' lives in random hotels in Asia, evading Trump supporters. toecomics.com

Reid Psaltis is a West Coast wanderer working as a science illustrator and making comics in his spare time. reidpsaltis.com

Marc Palm is a cartoonist / illustrator in Seattle where he creates strange and often disturbing images. He was the organizer of the *Intruder* comics newspaper.

Q: Geoffrey, you've just finished writing this book. What are you doing next?

A: I'm going to Busch Gardens in Williamsburg, Virginia!